Miracles and Mysteries of the Bible

Miracles and Mysteries of the Bible

A retelling of the glorious
Mysteries and Miracles
from both
Old and New Testaments

M.L. del Mastro

CASTLE BOOKS

This edition published in 2005 by

Castle Books ®

a division of Book Sales, Inc.
114 Northfield Avenue
Edison, NJ 08837

Copyright © 1987 by Castle Books

ISBN 13: 978-1-55521-228-5
ISBN 10: 1-55521-228-X

Printed in the United States of America

Contents

Preface   7

The Multiplication of the Loaves and Fishes   11

Walking on Water   21

Demoniac of the Geresenes   35

Jairus   60

Moses and the Sea of Reeds   76

The Centurion's Servant   112

The Paralyzed Man   123

Moses and the Burning Bush   135

The Canaanite Woman's Daughter   154

Preface

A miracle has been defined as a temporary suspension of the laws of nature by God, nature's creator, for purposes of His own. In the history of God's dealings with men, as recorded in the Judaeo-Christian tradition, this direct intervention with the day-to-day running of creation has happened rarely, and always with didactic purpose.

The Bible records many of these interventions, and wraps each in the context of the people on whose behalf the wonder was wrought, noting the lesson they learned (or failed to learn, fully), from the event, the reaction of the bystanders (some of whom suffered from the intervention), and the particular "element" of himself that God meant to reveal by this direct, dramatic encounter with men in their world.

In the Bible, the Scriptures held sacred by Jews and Christians, and seen by both as God's revelation of himself to men in word and deed, the wonders recorded gradually unfold a "picture" of God for those who approach with openness and reverence. Those who come with explicit faith find even greater riches, as they encounter the God that Scripture reveals.

It becomes clear to the reader tracing from the first records the power of God at work among men, that God uses his omnipotence in various ways. Some of these uses appear destructive, but in all these uses Israel, God's chosen race, selected to bring redemption to all mankind by means of a specially annointed leader (Messiah; in Greek Christos: in English, Christ), is drawn closer to him and taught the meaning of fidelity. By God's fidelity in protecting or rescuing his people from their enemies and their own frailties and failures, God teaches Israel how to keep the Covenant she has made.

As the dimensions of Covenant expand in Israel's

consciousness, so do the ramifications of fidelity--God's to Israel and Israel's to God. God makes further use of wonder through his prophets, both to teach Israel how to trust him as a loving Father, and to indicate to her, by concrete effects, the essential dangers to her of failing to trust him, "the only God there is."

The final form of Covenant between God and Israel, espousal ("As a young man approaches his bride, so shall your Builder wed you"), brings the last set of wonders, the espousal itself being the chief of them, from a philosophical and theological point of view. With this vision, and the injunction to wait in fidelity, the strictly Hebrew portion of Scripture ends.

From an examination of these miracles, all open-minded readers can profit, for they show forth God in His splendor and teach men his love for them and the glory that awaits them if they are faithful in waiting for his coming and in receiving him when, and as, he makes himself known.

The second, smaller section of the Bible, the New Testament, is the record made by his followers of the coming of the Messiah, Jesus of Nazareth. In this record of the life, works, sayings, death and rising of Jesus, and of the early life of his church, wonders or miracles take on the same didactic function they have had in the Old Testament. That is, they show forth, or serve as "signs" (John, the evangelist's only word for miracle) for, the active presence of God. They reveal the nature and attitudes of God toward men and they build a "new Covenant" or alliance, making espousal between God and man available to the whole of the human race.

In the "new Covenant", the omnipotence of God is exercised exclusively through his Messiah, His Christ, Jesus of Nazareth, and through Jesus, by His delegation of power, to the men He chose out from Israel to be his own emissaries.

For Christian readers, a study of these later "signs" reveals plainly that their worker, Jesus, was Son of God as well as Son of Man, that he was sent by God to redeem man from sin and reconcile him to the Father, and that, upon dying by crucifixion, rising from the dead and ascending to his Father in Heaven, he sent to his followers the Holy Spirit, God, who continued to work wonders through the Apostles and early Christians for the same purposes for which Jesus had worked them. (Throughout the manuscript where "man" appears, it is used in the sense of the Latin homo, meaning humankind, or universal humanity. Only where particularization is necessary to the discussion are the masculine and feminine prounouns used, as appropriate to the context).

For the reader who is not a Trinitarian Christian, or who does not accept the divinity of Jesus, the Christ, the miracles still "sign" in concrete deeds the revelation of God as love and of his faithful care for all men.

For the Jew who still waits (the Christian might say, on the far side of a "time warp"), for the coming of the Messiah, the fulfillment of God's espousal of Israel, and the ensuing redemption of the world, these later miracles not in his scriptures can open the mind, the imagination and the heart to the possibilities of love and healing beyond human scope, and in so doing, prepare him to receive his God when he comes.

What this book proposes to do is to reexamine, or perhaps retell would be a more correct word, a selection of the miracles of the Bible from the point of view of the persons who were their beneficiaries. This alteration in perspective from that found in Scripture has several advantages.

In the first place, while the miracles in both halves of Scripture were wonders wrought for public instruction and communal comfort or warning, each also had a private, individual communication. After all, God act-ed upon, through or on behalf of a particular man or woman with a personal history and a unique relationship, both to other people and to God himself, by virtue of this individuality. It was this individual who had the direct, immediate experience of God's presence, power and love and responded as a private unique individual. The private communications underlying the miracles recorded had relevance only to the person involved, just as the "shorthand" emotional communications between lovers are incomprehensible to the rest of the world, and so are not usually given public utterance.

The fact that these communications between God and the miracle's beneficiary were not recorded is useful in that it frees the imagination and the heart to work with the mind in reconstructing the event. One may use what is known of the times, customs and people, and draw as well upon universal, emotional and psychological truths in making the reconstruction, without altering or challenging the Scriptural text. In other words, these retellings simply try to supply a ruefully described deficiency of recorded history, which "never tells you what you really want to know about anyone or anything", without betraying the truth that is revealed and recorded.

A third value of this approach to the Bible's miracles is that the receptive reader may do independently what this writer has had the joy of doing--opening a door and entering into the presence of God at work among men. Reading an imaginative reconstruction by one person of another person's recorded, but not annotated, encounter with God can tap intellectual, imaginative and emotional resources in the reader. The reader then may, on the basis of personal experience and intuitive insight see still other possibilities and ramifications in this miracle, or in others, which may serve as a key, allowing God to reveal himself at deeper levels of experiential reality, and the reader to receive, enter into and respond to this revelation with deeper faith, hope and love than may ever have been possible before. That, at any rate, is the intention, the hope and the prayer of the writer for anyone willing to share in this journey into the Bible to relive its miracles and enter its mysteries.

The Multiplication of the Loaves and Fishes

The day had been hot, and in that milling crowd, dusty, but Aaron had not minded, much. He was a slender lad, tall for ten years old, with his mother's dark hair and eyes, and her responsive mouth. His jaw was his father's, though, strong and well-formed, jutting forward a bit when he had made up his mind to something. "A perfect mule," his grandmother fumed to his patient mother, more frequently and more loudly than she need have done to make her point, as her daughter-in-law very occasionally reminded her. Though Aaron privately agreed with his grandmother, and knew his mother did too, neither judgement had any effect on his decisions, once taken. As long as Aaron did not extend his attempts at independence to his apprenticeship with his father, Jonah supported them, mostly by silence, and when necessary, by a flat refusal to intervene in "women's matters."

Aaron's presence on this mountainside this late afternoon in early April had been the result of one of his independent decisions, taken with his father's consent over his grandmother's and mother's objections. Aaron grimaced slightly as he recalled the, well, discussion after supper the previous evening.

His grandmother had broached the issue to her son as Aaron, silent but mutinous and determined, sat listening. "Surely, Jonah, you're not going to let Aaron go traipsing off to listen to that rabble-rousing carpenter from Nazareth: I'm sure you have too much work for him to do at the shop to be able to spare him for such gallivanting. Besides, he's--" and she had broken off. Just in time, too, Aaron reflected with the trace of a grin. As he, and his father, too, well knew, she had been about to add, "... much too young to go off by himself," and had only just stopped herself in time.

She had remembered that, as Jonah's apprentice, he was actually, if not officially, past his childhood, and, though until his Bar Mitzvah he might have to travel with the women and children when a family group went on an extended journey, his behavior was now under his father's control. Anything he did during the day was his father's responsibility, and if Jonah chose to allow him to go, neither his mother nor his grandmother, formidable though these women were, would dare to oppose him. Until Jonah spoke, however, they felt free to air their arguments. And Jonah had not yet spoken.

Aaron waited tensely, watching his mother, who seemed prepared, as she usually was, to second her mother-in-law. He could not speak himself until, and unless, his father asked him to, and if his mother's arguments were effective, his father might decide the issue without even hearing Aaron's side of it.

Aaron had mentioned to his father as they were working with the new hides, the possibility of his being allowed to go to hear and see the wonderworker, Jesus of Nazareth. But Jonah, preoccupied with the difficulties the hides were presenting, had merely grunted non-commitally and given him some urgent directions about the handling of his section of the hide.

Aaron had worked with his father long enough to understand that then was not the time to pursue the matter of Jesus and his own day off. He had concentrated, instead, on the work at hand, confident that, once work had ended and the evening meal was over, he would have time to explain to his father why it was so important to him to be able to see this miracle-worker with his own eyes and to hear what he had to say.

But somehow his grandmother had gotten wind of

his project, how he did not know, had openly disapproved of if, and was turning to her daughter-in-law to command her support.

And then, before his wife could speak or his mother catch her breath and regroup after her near-error in tactics, Jonah had turned to his son with a quizzical look. "Well, Aaron?" he had said, and the tone was ironic, but grounded in warm affection. "Perhaps you can justify the loss to me of a full day of your invaluable services as my only apprentice at the shop?"

"Yes, father!" The boy had all but shouted his joyous response, then hastily lowering his voice and composing himself, had repeated more quietly, "Yes, father, I can."

"Very well, then. That's settled." Jonah had said, so swiftly that both the eloquence that had been about to pour from his excited son and the objections that had threatened to flood from his wife and mother had been cut off before anyone could draw breath. "You'll want to be off early," the father had added smoothly, "and I don't suppose you'll be home until after dark, so be sure to take along something substantial to eat. Mother and Grandmother will be glad to pack you plenty, I'm sure!"

With his last words, Jonah had shifted his eyes from Aaron, first to his wife and then to his mother, and while his voice had remained mild and somewhat speculative, neither woman had missed the command in his glance, and without a word they dropped their eyes and their objections together. They had packed Aaron a sack of food that would have satisfied three boys his age "going off into the wilderness like that" as they thought of the expedition. Essentially, they were generous, nurturing women.

And so here he was, clutching at the sack with what was left of his food, at the sunset of that day he had spent, with several thousand others, in the company of Jesus and his friends. He had been pushed up close to the inner circle of Jesus' disciples both by the pressure of the shifting crowds and by the use of his own determined ingenuity and lithe body. He could, he had discovered, slip between people where a full-grown man could not have moved an inch, and he had reached "the Twelve," as he had heard someone call them, soon after the crowd left Bethsaida, following Jesus.

Aaron had heard every word Jesus had said. It had all been wonderful. He had the feeling that his head was about to explode, so full had it become of all this marvelous teaching, and he was beginning to wish that he could make everything stop, just for a few minutes, so that he could make a start at getting all these teachings into some kind of order.

At that point, Jesus, having come to a stopping place in his discourse, suddenly gestured, and his Twelve at once gathered around him. Aaron moved in with them, scarcely aware of what he was doing. He had learned some of their names during the course of the day, and had been spoken to more than once by the friendly one they called Andrew. Andrew, it seemed was the brother of the blustering Simon, whom everyone called by the Greek nickname the Master had given him, "Rocky". It was to Andrew that Aaron attached himself as the group drew together around Jesus, and Andrew placed a reassuring hand on his shoulder.

The Master looked at them all, but spoke directly to Philip, the friend of Nathaniel, or Bartholomew as he was usually called.He asked,

"Where shall we buy bread for these people to eat?" (John 6:5)

Philip looked blank. He glanced briefly at his equally nonplussed companions, then back to Jesus. Surely Jesus was not serious? But evidently he was. And he was waiting for an answer. Before Jesus had to repeat this question, Philip, glancing around at the crowd, gave the obvious response.

"Not even with two hundred days' wages could we buy loaves enough to give each of them a mouthful!" (John 6:7)

Philip looked around the circle of Twelve again and

was a little relieved to see his companions nodding. After all, there must be five thousand or so, and that wasn't counting the women or the children. How could they, poor men all, find money enough to feed this crowd? One of the Twelve suggested hesitantly,

"This is a deserted place and it is already late. Why do you not dismiss them so that they can go to the cross roads and villages around here and buy themselves something to eat?" (Mark 6:35-36)

It was a sound suggestion as far as it went, thought Aaron, moving a little closer to Andrew, but he himself had no money to buy food, and he knew that some of the people who had left Bethsaida with them that morning were equally short of cash. He said a quick thank-you to God for his father's thoughtfulness in instructing his mother and grandmother to pack food for him. He added another thanks that his mother's and grand- mother's anxiety for his safety and their disapproval of the rash project had been translated, at his father's command into the lunch even he had not been able to finish.

And then Aaron had his idea. How much was left of his provisions? He had to squirm a bit to get his left hand into the sack to feel around, because the crowd had been steadily pressing in on its center. Aaron found that, though the cheese and figs had long since vanished, he still had two dried fish and five small loaves of barley bread, hand-sized for eating in haste. He withdrew his hand and reached out to tug at Andrew's sleeve, to get the kindly man's attention.

"What is it lad?" asked the friend of Jesus, taking his eyes from the Master to look down with some concern at the engaging and serious youngster who seemed to have become his second shadow for the day. "What's the trouble?"

"Nothing. Only, I have some food left that mother and grandmother packed for me. It's good--five barley loaves and two dried fish. Maybe the Master would like them? He must be hungry. He hasn't eaten anything all day, and I've had the whole rest of the sack."

Andrew smiled at Aaron and turned back to convey the boy's offer to Jesus. But Jesus was speaking again, apparently in response to the last suggestion.

"There is no need for them to disperse. Give them something to eat yourselves." (Matthew 14:16)

The Twelve were stunned. How were they to obey this command? In ironic disbelief, one of them snorted,

"Are we to go and spend two hundred days' wages for bread to feed them?"

"How many loaves have you?" Jesus asked. "Go and see." (Mark 6:37-38)

As the others were turning to each other in confusion, Andrew moved forward bringing Aaron with him. Smiling, he placed the boy in front of him and said to Jesus,

"There is a lad here who has five barley loaves and a couple of dried fish, but what is that for so many?" (John 6:9)

Jesus looked from Andrew to Aaron, with attention. He seemed tired, the boy thought, drained of energy. There were dark circles under his eyes, and beneath the weathered tan, his skin was almost gray. It had been a very long day, and Jesus had never once stopped in teaching the people. Aaron, extending the open sack to Jesus, hoped he would eat something, and maybe sit down for a while.

Then Jesus, still looking into Aaron's eyes, smiled warmly. It was as if the world had stopped for a second, caught its breath, and burst into flower and birdsong. Aaron was stunned with the force, but not in the least frightened. He felt warm and completely loved, in this gaze that seemed to penetrate to the core of his being, seeing everything in Aaron there was to see, and cherishing it all. Aaron had never felt such love in his life. All he knew was that, no matter what, he never wanted Jesus to look away, and he never wanted to be out of range of those wonderful, caring eyes.

And then Jesus was taking the sack from him, instructing the Twelve to get the people to sit down in groups on the grass. The Twelve moved through the crowd passing on the Master's instructions, and fairly soon the whole five thousand or so had settled down

"In hundreds and fifties, neatly arranged like flower beds," (Mark 6:40)as Peter, talking years afterward to his friend Mark, would recollect.

The people all turned toward Jesus, as flowers turn toward the sun, and waited to see what he would do. Aaron, still standing in front of him, saw him reach into the sack for the loaves and fish. He gave the sack back to Aaron who took it almost unconsciously, so intent was he upon this wonderful Jesus.

And then the Master spoke. With the five small loaves and two fish in his hands, he "raised his eyes to heaven, pronounced a blessing over them and gave them to his disciples for dis-tribution to the crowd." (Luke 9:16)

Aaron, still staring at Jesus, bemused, came back to the present with a start as Andrew, carrying his supply of bread and fish for the crowd, pressed three half-loaves and a fish into Aaron's hands."That's too much," the boy began to protest, when he looked at what Andrew was carrying. His friend must have twenty half-loaves and two dozen fish, the boy calculated. Then he noticed that each of the Twelve, similarly laden, was hurrying into his own sector of the crowd, giving each person as much as he wanted.

Chewing on one of his half-loaves, Aaron looked around the crowd. He noticed that everyone was getting plenty to eat, and that the supplies in the hands of the distributors never seemed to diminish.

But that was impossible! There had only been five loaves and two fish to begin with! How were all these people being fed, and satisfied, out of that? The food they were eating was certainly real. The crust in Aaron's hand and the fish in his mouth attested to that. But how?

Aaron turned back to look for Jesus. There stood the Master, by himself, still standing at the center of the now-seated crowd. Somehow, Aaron reflected, he looked different. He was certainly not less tired than he had been when he had thought about getting food for the people who had followed him so far. Nor had he eaten any of the bread and fish that he had given the disciples to give the crowd--his bread Aaron remembered, but that had only been the starting point. So he must still be hungry. Yet Aaron could see no trace in him either of exhaustion or of hunger. Instead, there was a quiet satisfaction, a repose of spirit that radiated from Jesus like the light of a lamp in a dark room, or the warmth of a fire on a chilly night.

He must have done it, Aaron realized. Jesus must have made bread and fish where there was neither bread nor fish in that quantity to be had! And why? So that the people who had followed him might not have to go hungry. As if it was his responsibility to care for his followers, rather than their privilege to care for him and provide for his needs! Aaron had never heard of anyone who really cared this way about other people, people whose only tie to him, as far as the boy could tell, was that they, like Aaron, wanted to stay near Jesus, to hear what he had to say, and had found food much less important than listening to him when it came to a choice between the two.

At that point, Jesus seemed to come back from wherever he had been. He surveyed the people, and, seeing them replete, content with the meal, he combed the crowd for his friends with his eyes, summoning each of them to his side with the touch of a single, accurate glance. Aaron, reattaching himself to Andrew and moving back to Jesus, heard him say to the Twelve

"Gather up the crusts that are left over, so that nothing will go to waste." (John 6:12)

The Twelve fanned out again through the still-seated crowds, making improvised baskets of their cloaks. Aaron used his lunch sack, but that soon overflowed and he had to empty it into Andrew's bulging cloak, and to content himself with helping his friend in collecting the scraps. The two worked their way back to

Jesus, and, one by one, the others, similarly laden, joined them.

Twelve basketfuls of leftovers out of five small loaves and two dried fish! Aaron was stunned. He wasn't alone. No one could seem to credit what had happened, and the noise of the crowd rose from a murmur to a roar. Glancing quickly around, Jesus realized that, unless he took charge, the crowd would become a mob, and, seizing him for their figurehead-king, would charge upon the established government to overthrow it, and that was not why he had come.

At once he acted. He sent the protesting Twelve to the boat to set out without him; he would meet them on the other side of the lake. Then, moving from group to group before the people could themselves rise, he dismissed each group with a blessing. He moved quickly, but without apparent haste, and, as Aaron watched, he heard the incipient roar break up and be reduced to a confused murmur. It was late, and the people began to hurry in twos and threes toward the roads that would take them to their own villages.

As Aaron stood watching, his eyes still fixed on Jesus as he moved expertly through the crowd sending the people on their separate ways home, he felt a hand on his shoulder. He turned and found Andrew, the last of the Twelve still left at the crowd's rapidly disappearing center. "I must go with the others," Andrew told him, "and you'd best be on your way too. Do you know how to get home again?"

"Yes," said Aaron. "There were several people from my street here." He looked to his left. "There's one now. Simeon" he called, and the graying man who had been looking around the crowd, turned, saw the boy and started toward him. "I'll go with him," said Aaron to Andrew.

"Fine then," Andrew agreed. "I must be off. But here. Take some of these leftovers with you. After all, they were your loaves and fish to begin with!" And smiling, Andrew filled Aaron's sack with some of what the two had gathered. "Perhaps you'll come to hear

Jesus again?" he added, and there was a hope in the question that made it an invitation.

"Oh yes!" Aaron breathed, his desire blazing in his eye, his face, his whole being. "Jesus is--wonderful!"

"Good," said Andrew, and then to Simeon, "You'll see the lad gets safely home?"

"So I promised his father when he asked me to keep an eye out for him!" the older man assured him. Aaron jumped, and stared at Simeon shocked. Simeon smiled at him. "You didn't know that? Well, I guess your father wanted you to be on your own for a bit, and find your own way if you had to, but without leaving you in any real danger. That's like Jonah," he added, looking at Andrew, who nodded his comprehension. He smiled at Simeon and Aaron, and hurried to catch up to his brother, Simon "Rocky", who was bellowing for him to "get a move on it! We haven't got all night!"

"Well, lad, we'd best be off, too!" said Simeon at last, and, as Aaron nodded, his mind and heart too full for conversation just then, the two set off for the village. They walked together companionably, dipping into Aaron's sack of leftover bread and fish, and eating as they walked.

Walking on Water

Simon, son of John and senior partner in the informal fishing group he and his brother Andrew had formed with the sons of Zebedee, James and John, flung an impatient look over his shoulder. Where was that brother of his now! The other ten of the Twelve had already stowed their loads of leftover bread and fish, wrapped in cloaks and whatever else had come to hand as they had gathered up the remains of Jesus' feast, and had taken their places in the boat. All was in readiness for them to shove off the beach and head back to Bethsaida and Capernaum, as the Master had commanded--except that Andrew and his cloak full of bread and fish had not yet arrived. Where had he gotten to?

Simon, never a patient man, was fuming at the delay. Once he had started to do something or to go somewhere, he did not like to have the action interrupted, whatever the cause. But in this case, until Andrew showed up--and where was he?--there was nothing he could do. He checked the stowage of the bread and fish again, and reminded himself that they'd better take a little extra care with the oars or the food would get wet and be spoiled, and Jesus had had them gather it up just to prevent such waste.

As the small, usually unheeded, voice in the back of his awareness repeated to him, for the fifth or sixth time that afternoon, that he really ought to sit down some time soon, and think about that bread and fish, he caught sight of Andrew, speaking a last word to a man and a boy in the crowd and then turning toward shore. He was walking, but without haste, and that snapped Simon's fragile control. "Come on!" he bellowed, and Andrew looked up, startled. "Get a move on it. We haven't got all night!" he continued in an aggrieved shout that startled the shore birds, though the men in the boat, used to his short fuse and explosive temper, simply grinned at one another.

Andrew got a move on it at once, and arrived at the boat on the run. "Stick your stuff in and let's get out of here!" commanded Simon, already shin deep in the water on the boat's port side, hands on the gunwale, ready to shove the boat free of the sand. Andrew, murmering his not very apologetic, "Sorry, I got held up!" gave his burden of bread and fish to John and grabbed the starboard gunwale opposite Simon. Together they heaved the boat free and scrambled aboard each on his own side. The routine, from years of practice, was entirely familiar and the brothers, though opposite in temperament and instinct, worked so completely as one in it that the boat didn't even wobble as they took their places.

A few strokes of the oars took them safely off shore and they settled to the hard work of the crossing. The sea of Galilee was thoroughly familiar to all the fishermen among them. They knew its moods, its sudden squalls, and its deceptive peacefulness as well as they knew one another's. Tonight, and reflected Simon grimly, it was night now, thanks to Andrew's dilly-dallying, the sea was smooth as the grass on the hillside had been. Though this flat calm was itself ominous, portending storm usually, he hoped it would stay that way, at least for their crossing. A little breeze might feel good as they worked the oars, but on the Sea no breeze could be trusted to stay little. Once, even a small wind began it sometimes seemed to listen to the sound of its own motion and become drunk on it. Then it could feed on itself, whipping itself up into a rage and a roar like a thing possessed--or like himself when he lost his temper, Simon wryly admitted to himself with a slight grimace. Somewhat ashamed, he looked up to encounter the watching eyes of Andrew, who said at once, "I am sorry. But I had to find the boy whose bread and fish the Master used, to make sure he could get home again."

Simon nodded, knowing Andrew had read and accepted the apology his eyes, though not his mouth, had been able to make. "You gave him some of the bread and fish to take home?" The question was really a statement, for Simon knew Andrew almost as well as Andrew knew him.

"Yes," Andrew confirmed. "And a neighbor of his was there. The boy's father had asked him to keep an eye out for the lad, but unobtrusively. He showed up at the end and they went off home together."

Simon was satisfied, indeed pleased. A childless man himself, he liked spunky youngsters, but was not comfortable with them and hid so effectively behind his brusqueness that most of them were glad to keep out of his way. Andrew now, Andrew was different. Children were drawn to him. Wherever they were, by themselves, with the Twelve or in a mob like today's, whatever children there were who had come enough into their own personhood to separate themselves from their families and talk to people by themselves wound up attached to Andrew to his evident delight. Simon shook his head slightly. He had no idea how Andrew did it, but he admired his brother's skill and was pleased to have the children even that near.

"Simon? I mean Rocky?" The voice which sounded worried belonged to Matthew, new to the Twelve and still awkward with the Master's nickname for Simon. Levi, the ex-tax collector, was a thoroughgoing landsman, Simon remembered with a half-smile. Nice enough fellow, and honest too, though he was smart as anything about coinage, weights and measures and all the "city things" Simon himself mistrusted. The senior partner was shrewd about the Sea, boats, men and fish, but these slick-talking sharpers were another matter. Jesus had picked Matthew Levi Himself, though, and Simon Peter had quickly seen past the city skills to the man of integrity beneath them. With that man he had felt a bond of sympathy and kinship beginning to grow, rising out of their mutual but quite different appreciation of, love for, and loyalty to, the Master.

"Rocky?" came Matthew's voice again, and the edge of fear glinted like a knife drawn in the moonlight.

"What's up Matthew?" The current of concern in Simon's voice, riding strong under its usual bluster, gripped the other like a warm, strong hand on the shoulder and he relaxed a bit. "Does that cloudbank blocking out the stars over there mean anything?" he asked more calmly, almost apologetically. He had taken a lot of teasing for his innocent questions in these past weeks from the fisherman among Twelve to whom the Sea was a second home.

"Where?" asked Simon.

"Over there," he replied, pointing, and then, realizing that in the darkness Simon probably could not see the gesture added, "on the sta... por... left, toward the front of the boat."

"Port bow," Simon supplied absently as he scanned the night sky. He stiffened slightly. "Mmmph!" The exclamation was half smothered. The Twelve, who had been alerted to the seriousness of Matthew's question by the lack of immediate response from the usually volatile "Rocky," had looked for themselves, and echoed his grunt with an indrawn breath. Matthew wanted to speak again, if only to hear familiar voices in the alien, now threatening dark, but the quality of the silence around him bade him hold his tongue and he did.

"Trouble, I think," suggested John, Zebedee's younger son, and his brother James agreed. "I'll say. We've come too far to beat that back?" The question was really a declaration; it was a forlorn hope that made of it a weak interrogative.

"Yes." Simon's tone was flat, all but seamanship and rapid calculation erased from it. Matthew, listening, his fear tethered but not vanquished, suddenly understood that "Rocky" was "Rock" indeed, and saw without difficulty why he was senior partner both of the fishing group and of the Twelve. The Master in naming him had simply been putting the operative reality in Simon's character into words. "Rocky" was a man you were glad to have with you in a tight place, and from what the rest of the Twelve were saying, and not saying, it was plain that they were in a very tight place.

"So?" It was James again. "Ahead's no good. We'll be rowing into the wind."

"What wind?" Matthew wondered silently. So far there was none. The sea around them was flat as the water in a purification jar, or that in the sheep-pool at Bethesda when no angel was there to stir it up to heal the sick who waited there.

"But not for a while yet," John offered eagerly. "We could probably get pretty near Capernaum, or pretty nearly back to shore for that matter, if we pushed it a bit." John was always impetuous, always the optimist, Matthew remembered, aware even from his short tenure with the Twelve that John's youthful en-thusiasms usually served to rouse the more con-servative strains in the others, sometimes the tax-collector suspected, simply because they wanted to swat him as one does a frisky dog that has joggled his elbow and made him misfire with the wineskin, covering his tunic instead of filling his mouth.

This time, however, there was no annoyance, no snapping in the response. John had proposed the only possible course of action open to them, and they would have to consider it, like the manner or not.

"Which way then?" It was Andrew, the peace-maker, who seemed to have no problems getting along with anyone.

"Not back," offered Thomas, who was a twin, and was sometimes so addressed. "The Master said He'd meet us across the lake. He'll be expecting us to be at Capernaum, not to come back to where we left him. He wouldn't still be there, and then we'll have an awful time finding Him."

"He's not a seaman, remember," said Philip, Andrew's friend. "He won't understand why we're not at Capernaum when he gets there, and well, He'll be annoyed with us."

"I don't think--" John objected loudly, quickly to defend his beloved Master from any hint of criticism, but he was forestalled by Simon.

"No," Rocky declared, "He won't be angry, and He will understand. But he wants us with Him at Capernaum. That's where he'll have headed, and we have no way to let him know we won't be there. He might be worried. We can't get back anyway, so we'd better go on--and double the pace."

"Right!" John was cheerful again and while the men shifted places to let fresh rowers take over, he punched his brother James as the latter edged carefully passed him. "Attaway!" he crowed, and James answered him with a grin and a rough hand touseling his head.

"Save it for the oars!" James advised. "That's going to be some wind when it gets here!"

Matthew looked at "his" cloud bank again and all but gasped aloud. The speed with which this apparently monstrous storm was traveling defied belief--at least so it looked to a landsman. He found himself pressed against Andrew in the shift of positions and asked softly, "It really is a bad storm, and coming fast, isn't it?"

"Don't worry," Andrew reassured him. "It'll be nasty, all right, but this boat's lived through worse, and with only the two of us and a full load of fish. We'll be all right. Wet though," he added.

"My grandmother always says, 'You can't get wetter than wet,'" Matthew offered, in an attempt to shove his rising fear back down to where it belonged, and Andrew, recognizing both the fear and the steely attempt to conquer it, chuckled appreciatively.

"She's right--and in this case, the wind'll dry you off."

Then they settled to work in earnest, trying to make as much headway as they could before they met the oncoming storm. With their efforts the greater dark of the shores came appreciably nearer in a short time.

"Mile to go?" asked John between strokes.

"Nearer two," answered his brother James and looked to Simon for confirmation. "Rocky?"

"Two I'd say," declared the senior partner and then with a whoop and a roar, the storm was upon them, blotting out stars, shore and almost the sea itself. The wind was blowing at gale force and it whipped the relatively shallow lake into towering waves that crashed in upon them, tossing the boat and beginning to fill it. At Simon's wordless direction they headed the boat into the wind, and doubled up, two to an oar, to try to hold the boat steady as Matthew and Thomas began to bail. Then came the rain in horizontal sheets that all but cut the skin. It seemed to come from every direction at once as did the waves. Experienced fishermen though they were and knowledgeable about the Sea's sudden storms, the oarsmen had difficulty keeping the beleaguered craft headed upwind, while the bailers strove mightily just to keep it afloat.

Forward progress was, of course, impossible, Matthew soon concluded. The best they could hope for was to avoid capsizing, for in the seas this storm had raised they would drown without a trace. Drowning was a death he did not want to think about just then, so Matthew concentrated on bailing faster, trying to get ahead of the waves and the rain in their apparent determination to fill the boat like a cup.

He could not have said how long he had been at work. He had bailed with his right hand until his shoulders refused to lift his arm and then switched to the left. When the left gave out he had gone back to the right. It was the only contribution he could make to their joint safety and he was determined to continue until--well, just until.

And so he did. And now it was, how much later? He could not calculate. Time had somewhere acquired an elasticity, and each moment of it stretched out endlessly in front of him. Bend. Scoop. Lift. Toss. Bend. Scoop. . . . and so it went. It had been the whole of his life. It was all there would ever be.

Matthew had passed the point of fatigue long since, though he did not know it. All he noticed was that everything--boat, storm, sea, companions--everything but the bailer (which had become the natural extension of one or the other of his two arms) had receded somewhat. It had not faded into a dream, but it was not right on top of him either. The distancing was not unpleasant, but not comforting either. Somewhere far within him an alarm was sounding, but that too was distant, muffled, somehow less than real.

The storm, however, had not abated. Indeed in its fury, it had grown even fiercer, though to the battling men such an intensification had hardly seemed possible. Still they held the boat steady, rowing with all their strength into the wind and helping each other at the oars.

At about three in the morning, so Simon, the Rock, calculated, the storm, impossibly, unleashed a new fury of wind and rain. Inch by grudging inch, the boat began to slip backwards. At first the laboring men did not notice the shift. The oarsmen were far too pre-occupied with bending forward and angling the shared oars back into whatever of sea was, for the instant, flat enough for them to bite into. To "catch a crab," usually only humiliating and an occasion for some raucous teasing, was, in this situation, a real danger to rowers and craft.

It was Matthew, with his eye and brain thoroughly trained to estimate any profit or loss at a glance who, even in this unfamiliar world made almost surreal by the storm first noticed the slippage. "Tom?" into the ear of his fellow-bailer, "aren't we losing ground--er, I mean, sort of going backwards?"

Thomas shook his head and shrugged his shoulders. "Can't tell!" he bellowed back. "Bail!" And Matthew bailed.

But Simon, the Rock, had caught a part of the question and begun to look for himself, even as he heaved at his oar. The wash of water past the boat was what must have alerted Matthew, he thought, and Simon, looking down, saw the telltale evidence of what would soon be the deadly truth. They were slipping backwards, though so far, they had managed to stay upwind and relatively upright. But the wind and storm were gaining on them and with their increasing weariness, would gain more and more quickly. Once the storm had snatched the control of the craft from them, it would capsize them, and the backward drift was the first step in the deadly shift in the balance of powers. To Simon, it looked very much as though this would be their last battle for lives and boat against the Sea. His lips tightened and his shoulders squared as he settled himself more firmly in position to apply full strength to the task of rowing. They might lose this one, but it wouldn't be for lack of a fight.

Andrew, always aware of his brother's changes of mood looked over, puzzled. What had bitten Simon now? His eye could not catch Simon's, and for Andrew that was the invariable signal that they were in real trouble. Simon had a habit of keeping really grim news to himself--on grounds, Andrew had always supposed, (though he had never quite dared to confirm his guess), that if all that could be done was worry, the fewer who had to the better. Seeing that Simon had withdrawn into the core of his being and had completely focused his energies on the rowing with what amounted to a kind of rage, Andrew glanced quickly around what he could see of the boat. Nothing, nothing amiss, he looked back to the water running beside the boat. He could see it easily now--too easily, for it was nearly up to the gunwales. In spite of Matthew and Thomas, the boat was riding visibly lower and the waves crashing over it had been filling it rapidly.

And the water was running backwards. Andrew shook his head to clear it. Backwards? Had they been blown in a half circle, then? No--No. The wind had just increased so much that now it was in charge, or almost so, and was blowing them back the way they had come. All their rowing could no longer even keep them in place, and it was an open question how long it could keep them headed upwind.

Andrew calculated swiftly. They had been working hard since midnight, after a full day on land and an evening's rowing on the Sea before the storm. Simon ("Rock" was the right name for him. thought Andrew with a fleeting and appreciative grin) had seen the sign. That was plain. Had anyone else? The bailers maybe? He looked. Yes, they had. He caught Levi's eye and tried to smile, but it didn't quite work, and Matthew turned back, shaken, to his bailer and tried to double his rate--scoop-lift-toss-scoop. Andrew wanted to comfort him, but he knew he couldn't be heard, and anyway, what was there to say? They were going to die in this one, and that was that.

As if he had voiced his despairing conclusion aloud, the other rowers shifted a little. Some glanced at each other; the rest peered at the water now rushing swiftly past the boat. Only Simon and Nathaniel on the port side and Andrew with Philip on the starboard kept on rowing, as, pair by pair, the others lifted, then shipped their oars. The wind, for once, did not shift direction, and the bow of the boat stayed pointed where the rowers had placed it. "That's it!" shouted James, Zebedee's older son, his oar in the boat. "We've bought it this time."

John looked at him for a horrified, endless moment, then swung around to find the Rock's hooded eyes. "Well?" The question rang out in a sudden lull, while the storm seemed to catch its breath. "What--?" The rest of the question was swallowed by the gale as it swept down upon them, but Simon, as he looked up, confirmed their fears. He simply shrugged, and went on rowing, powerfully but mechanically. It was all there was to do. Pair by pair the others turned back to their oars, unshipped them and began again to row. It was useless, but it was better than doing nothing.

And then there was a small sound, that would have been a scream had the screamer had a breath to make one. It was John. His rowing partner, Simon the Zealot, his brother James and his fishing partners Simon the Rock and Andrew swiveled toward him at the sound--and they too caught their breath and screamed in disordered shock, terror and exhaustion. The shrieks alerted the rest who froze, then turned as one man to the spot to which John, now on his feet rigid and still gasping out shrieks of terror, pointed.

It was Jesus. He was walking in their direction but at an angle, so that if he kept on he would go right past them. But he was walking on the towering waves, his cloak and tunic whipped by the wind as he came. The waves threatened at every step to swallow him, but somehow as he put down each foot, the wave in front of it obediently flattened out, becoming a kind of floor for him-- as solid, reflected the bemused Matthew, as the stone floor of the courtyard where he used to set up his tax-collector's table. Matthew was too tired to think, to scream, so tired that he regarded even this terrifying phenomenon from that dangerous distance which had made of his companions and situation shadowy semirealities. The voices of his companions cut through his bemused fog. "Ghost!" they were screaming. "It's a ghost! Ghost! Ghost!" The screams reached a crescendo that topped the deafening howl of the wind, and Matthew, his mouth opening in a formless shriek, felt the hair rise on his head.

"Get hold of yourselves!" The voice was that of Jesus, the beloved Master. As he turned from his course and began to come toward them, his voice cut through the rising hysteria of the Twelve as it cut through the storm wind, in a single stroke, its command of both effortless and complete. He walked calmly toward the still laboring craft, which, with its oarsmen disabled by their fright, was now in truth very near capsizing. "It is I," he continued as he walked. "Don't be afraid."

At the reassuring strength and absolute authority of his voice, the oars dipped back into the raging sea and steadied the craft. Matthew and Thomas at once began to bail again. The storm had not abated a breath of its fury, the waves continued to break over the boat and the water continued to rush past it the wrong way, but the terror was gone as though it had never existed, and the Twelve knew, though they did not know how, that all would be well.

It was Simon the Rock who first recovered his voice

and, with it, both his leadership and his natural cau-
tion. "Lord,"he shouted to Jesus over the roar of the
wind, "If it is really you, tell me to come to you across
the water!"

The audacity of the proposal caught Matthew like a
blow to the diaphragm. Yet he knew, though the
others, from their stunned expressions, seemed not to,
why Simon was making this test of the apparition.
Matthew, too, was a tester of appearances--and he, too,
refused to give credence to a tale (or a vision; it was
really the same thing), however plausible, until he had
tested its truth for himself. No tax collector for the
Romans could hope to survive in Capernaum, he
reflected grimly, without a nose for a lie and a safety-
first check list to counteract all the ways a man could
be deceived by his own eyes and ears. Simon was
precisely right, he thought, even as he heard Jesus'
firm, "Come."

As though a wind had blown through his mind, the
fog he had been existing in had vanished, clearing his
senses. He watched awestruck, though he continued
automatically to bail, as the others, eyes also riveted on
Simon and Jesus, continued to row. Simon was
climbing out of the boat. He stood, stepped over the port
gunwale and onto the heaving surface of the storm
tossed sea.

As he put his left foot down, on a rising wave, the
others noticed, it flattened under its sole and supported
his full weight. It felt solid, Simon noticed, and steady
as dry land, though it was still water, wet to the touch.
He lifted his right foot from the thwart against which it
had been braced, brought it forward over the gunwale
and put it down in front of the left. the water under it
likewise grew solid, though the water continued to
whip wildly all around him and waves broke against
his calves and back while the wind's fury increased.

Simon looked toward the Master, who smiled slightly
and beckoned to him, nodding. Simon had moved four
more steps toward Jesus before he suddenly thought,
"What on earth am I doing out here? Suppose this is

an evil spirit, luring me to my death?" Panic rising, he glanced around him wildly and then back to the boat even as his right foot continued its forward motion to complete the fifth step. His eyes shot to Jesus and then to his descending right foot. He hesitated, and, as he put the foot down, a wave broke over the instep and he felt himself plunging in terror forward and down. His arms flung themselves into the air as the incomplete step took him from the surface of the sea on the way to its depths. He shouted as he plunged downward, "Lord, save me!" and tasted the water of the Sea as it filled his open mouth and washed over his nose.

At once he found himself standing again, on the surface of the sea, both his hands held firmly in Jesus's grasp. Jesus had wasted no time, Matthew noted, in moving the three steps it had taken him to reach his sinking "Rock," in grabbing the upstretched groping hands and in hauling the now-somewhat-shamefaced Simon back to the "floor" the water made under their feet.

Ascertaining that Simon had suffered no physical damage from his near-drowning in pursuit of the truth, Jesus, still holding both Simon's hands, said gently to him, "How little faith you have! Why did you falter?" And then, keeping Simon's right hand firmly caught in his left and placing Simon's still shaking left hand on his left forearm where it fastened itself involuntarily in a convulsive grip, Jesus put his right arm firmly around the shoulders of the stalwart leader of the Twelve and half-guided, half-carried him back to the boat.

Matthew, watching open-mouthed, breath held, saw both the effects of the shock visible on Simon's face and the genuine concern and love of Jesus for him as he handed the fisherman into the boat. Andrew and Simon the Zealot caught him as he stumbled and fell to his seat, while John eagerly reached over them to help Jesus get in. Of them all, thought Matthew, only John had no residual fear of Jesus after what they had seen him do. John's only anxiety was that Jesus might go away again, and the young fisherman looked ready to leap out of the boat to drag him in, with or without the inviatation of Jesus, rather than let that happen.

Looking at them all Jesus smiled and stepped over the gunwale into the boat. They had not yet fully made room for him, and Simon's teeth had not stopped chattering when two things happened. The storm ceased abruptly, with the winds becoming the mildest breeze and the mountainous waves flattening into gentle ripples, and the keel of the boat was grinding into the sands at their accustomed landing place near Bethsaida, but on the Capernaum side of the mouth of the Jordan.

There was a graying in the east; dawn would soon break. The twelve gathered themselves together, tired, bewildered and awestruck. Matthew heard broken murmurs from them as, gathering up their bundles of bread and fish and stowing boat gear, they glanced again and again toward the Master and quickly away. "Who . . . ?" and "How?" punctuated the murmer of sound as often as "God's favor," "the one?" and, more hesitantly "God's son?"

Then, bundles shouldered and boat secured, they gathered around Jesus, growing silent as they waited for his next direction.

Demoniac
of the Geresenes

At last the sun was about to rise. Jothan stretched himself and, experimentally, began to rise from the sheltered corner of the rock mound, a tomb, where he had spent a restless night. Actually, he couldn't remember much of what had happened to him, but he had the shadow of a memory that it had been a hard time, a very long period of darkness this time, over which his control had been as minimal as his remaining memory of the time passed. Gingerly he flexed his arms and turned his hands, palms up, palms down, checking for damage. Two nasty rock cuts on the left forearm, a gouge in the right upper arm that was still bleeding, and severe contusions beginning to swell and blacken on the right forearm, with the usual briar scratches lacing his hands and wrists--an average crop he reflected wryly.

Raising himself up on his right elbow, less sore than the left, he surveyed his legs. The right was bent under him, and he wondered if it had been broken. He pushed himself to a sitting position, straightening his right arm and, finally, bracing himself on the heel of his right hand, he carefully drew the bent right leg out from under the left, straightening it and gently rotating the foot. All seemed to be in working order, and no sharp stabs of pain greeted any of his movements. Probably, then, nothing was seriously damaged, this time.

Jothan sighed. He drew both feet, flat on the ground, toward his body, and with his back braced against the tomb, leaned forward, resting his head on his raised knees which he circled with his arms, clasping an elbow loosely with either hand. He could stand up, but what was the point?

There would be some food, left for him daily by some kindly person from the village, in front of one of the larger tombs, but Jothan wasn't hungry enough this morning to search the graveyard for it. He could never remember exactly which tomb it was that served his donor for a station, so he had to go to each one and walk all around it. Sometimes, he knew, he got confused, and he suspected he walked around some of the same tombs two and three times, coming at them from different angles.

When he did find the right tomb Jothan recognized it, but he never knew just how. It seemed to him that he also recognized the olive-wood cup, the gray bowl with its thin blue stripes that always held the soup, and the cleverly woven covered basket with its linen napkin over the small loaves of barley bread in one section and dried fish and hard cheese in two smaller sections, but again, he could not say why or how. He knew the cup, bowl and basket were always the same, and he sensed that whoever put them there every day was careful always to arrange them in exactly the same relation to each other and to the tomb, but there was some familiarity of the bowl and basket at least, beyond that, which continued to elude Jothan. And today he was too--well, tired, for want of a better word, to allow the mystery to tease him to pursue its solution.

So he sat, faced into the rising sun, his shoulders and neck bent forward to receive its warming rays, which would not become intolerable for some hours, and idly studied the ground between his freshly lacerated, well-scarred feet. What was the use of moving? What was the use of doing, or trying to do, anything at all?

Suddenly Jothan raised his head. He had felt the premonitory tightening in his gut and thighs that always signalled the start of one of his "attacks", as the people in the village were accustomed to call them. He was alarmed. He knew his sense of time was badly bent, but it seemed to him only moments since he had fallen in a heap beside the tomb, just emerged from an "attack" and wanting only peace. Was it to begin again?

Automatically he glanced at his hands and arms. Yes, the fingers were beginning to knot and curl, though his wounds were still bleeding from the last time. It was too soon. What was happening? Jothan tried to still the rising panic that always amplified the force and effects of the attacks on him. He had learned, by painful experimentation, that if he could disengage his own mind, will and emotions, his spirit, the process of the attack, while it damaged his body, would leave him relatively untroubled.

But that kind of detachment was difficult, and had its own cost; one of the effects of successful disengagement during an attack was profound disorientation after it was over, for he could recall neither what had happened during the attack nor what had gone before it.

In disengagement, his spirit was encased in a glass bubble, and nothing outside was ever quite real. Nevertheless if that bubble should be smashed--Jothan shuddered and focused his exhausted spirit on reconstructing the one shelter he had been able to make in the chaos that had been his world for so long.

Twenty yards away, from behind a large tomb, a boy of almost ten was observing Jothan. He was Timon, son of the swineherd Ethan. He liked to go with his father whenever he could, for the high ground above the Lake gave him a view of the countryside that could be had nowhere else.

Timon had first gone to the tombs when he came to the uplands to visit his father and the other herdsmen, the year before. At that time he had seen Jothan for the first time, half-naked and frenzied, running wildly through the area of the tombs. Timon had crouched behind a low mound, torn between fascination and terror, and watched, as Jothan, his wrists and ankles bloody, stripped off his filthy, torn clothing, flung it as far from him as he could, and ran as if he wished he could run out of his own body. He had lost his sandals somewhere, Timon concluded, for he had bare feet, and these were being cut and bruised as he crashed through the rocky area and careened off boulders and tombs. Finally, Timon saw, he grew exhausted and collapsed sobbing by the side of a tomb. There he lay, fighting for breath and holding onto the ground, so it had seemed to the wondering watcher, until with a great scream something seemed to tear a way out of him, leaving him in an exhausted, bleeding heap on the ground.

Cautiously, Timon had edged his way over to the now quietly sobbing, exhausted man. "Can I help you?" he had asked, tentatively, but without fear. Timon, eldest of five children of the swineherd had had more experience of suffering, his own and other people's, than most youngsters his age. He had learned, both from his father who cared for the beasts, and from his mother and grandmother who cared for him, for the rest of the family and for the village, the two truths about pain: that pain got its power to destroy the spirit only from fear of the pain, and that pain could often be eased if one went directly to the source of it to apply the proper remedy.

"Can I help you?" he had repeated, a little louder, when Jothan did not reply.

Finally the battered man had uncurled, rolled over and opened his rapidly swelling eyes. "I don't know," he croaked, barely able to move his mouth to speak. "I don't think so, but thank you."

Timon, surveying the wreckage, acted with his mother's efficiency and his grandmother's kindness. He took off the short cloak he had worn to the upland, rolled it into a pillow and wedged it between the man's head and the rocky ground. "Just stay there a bit," he said gently, his tone like his father's when the swineherd had to deal with a hurt beast, a hog usually, now; his father liked to say that hogs were essentially indestructible, unlike his former charges, the sheep, which, he said, were essentially self-destructive, silly and stupid, and very demanding of care and repair. Still, Timon noticed, Ethan did not like hogs very much and he had always liked the sheep, however much they annoyed him and however poorly herding them paid. Ethan had named them and knew them as individuals, as all good shepherds did. As he had explained to Timon, no two sheep were alike any more than two people were alike, however similar they might appear to be. Thinking of his mother and her mother, his grandmother, Timon understood.

He had reached the stream by this time and stripping off his tunic he tore it in wide strips and dipped them into the running water. Mother would be annoyed, he thought, even though this was his oldest tunic almost falling into holes, and he had really out-grown it, but Grandmother would understand.

Carefully, Timon made his way back to Jothan who had dropped into a feverish doze. The sun had begun to shine into Jothan's closed eyes and he made feeble attempts to rid himself of it. Timon looked around. If he could help the battered man move into the angle created by the tomb and the hillside, he would be sheltered from the sun and from the wind at night; he could huddle under the lee of the stone stopping the mouth of the tomb if the rains came,but that would not be for a while.

"Sir?" he said and Jothan stirred. "Sir? Can you move at all by yourself?" Jothan looked toward the voice, focusing with difficulty. "If you can," Timon continued, recognizing that the man's hold on consciousness was slipping fast, "come around to the side of the mound. Use my shoulder to help yourself up," he added and knelt on one knee next to Jothan. He stayed steady as a boulder until Jothan had heaved himself to his knees, leaning on Timon's shoulder, and then Timon, tucking the rolled cloak under one arm, rose. Jothan rose with him, and they moved around the side of the tomb to the shelter Timon had seen.

Once there, Jothan had collapsed and curled again into the protective position of a man guarding himself against more pain. Tucking the rolled cloak under Jothan's head, Timon took one of his soaked linen

strips and squeezed it carefully into Jothan's open
mouth, a few drops at a time. Jothan caught the end of
the strip in his mouth and began to suck greedily at it.
After getting the water from three more strips Jothan
relaxed and Timon was able to cleanse his wounds
with the still damp strips. He went back to the stream,
rinsed the strips and brought them back.

It took Timon six trips to the stream to get Jothan
cleaned of mud and blood, and on his seventh return he
carefully bound the worst of the wounds with the strips.
Then he sat back on his heels and surveyed the now-
sleeping man. All right for now, he concluded, but the
man would need care, food and clothing if not nursing,
for a good while to get well. He would have to consult
his father.

When Timon found Ethan and the swineherds his
father was concerned, though not, yet, angry. As always (and unlike his mother), Ethan asked questions
first and only after he had listened, really listened, to
the answers, meted out punishment if he felt it was
deserved. His mother, with quick hands to match a
flame-quick temper, tended to reverse the procedure.
Timon took his mother's outbreaks in stride, but truly
dreaded his father's wrath and went to extraordinary
lengths to avoid incurring it. Now he said, in response
to his father's quiet question, "At the tombs. Father?"

"Yes son?"

"Father, I saw a man up there, running into the
rocks and tombs and tearing off his clothes. He looked
really frightened, and he sounded so angry I thought
he was being chased. But he was all alone. He fell
down, finally beside a tomb and he just kept crying."

"Did you try to help him?" asked his father, as Seth,
an older herder, murmured "Jothan!"

"I did, sir," said Timon. Better to answer his
father's questions first. Later he would pursue Seth's
remark. "I put my cloak under his head so he
wouldn't bang it on the rocks anymore, and I got some
water from the stream to clean his wounds."

"That was an old tunic, I trust?" His father, leaning

forward, his mouth partly hidden by his hand, sounded odd, and Timon looked at him quickly but met only Ethan's usual serious look and kindly brown eyes. Ethan was not frowning, only, it appeared, curious, and Timon relaxed.

"Yes, sir," he replied. "It should have gone to Mark last month, but I persuaded Grandmother to let me keep it. It was so thin Mark would have had it in holes in a week, and Mama would have been upset with him. I knew I could get more wear out of it, and besides, it was finally getting soft enough to be comfortable.

"You won't get much more wear out of it, as things stand," remarked Ethan in that same strange tone.

"No, sir," Timon replied with a puzzled frown. "I tore it up to make bandages for the man. I wet them in the stream first and he was able to suck some water from them. He liked that. He was like Blackie's Speckle when he was just born, with the milk and the strip of linen, you remember?"

Ethan nodded. "Are you chilly, son?" he asked. Timon, looking down, suddenly realized he was standing in the middle of the group of swineherds wearing only his sandals and a loin cloth. He blushed but met his father's eyes and answered the question directly.

"A little sir, but only when I'm out of the sun. But that man is in the shade--and he has no clothes at all. With his wounds, he's a bit feverish, even now. When night comes-Father, he'll die! We have to do something!"

"What?" asked Ethan. He had taken his hand from his mouth, and his voice was back to its usual, flat, matter-of-fact tone, not unkind but not enthusiastic. Steady, reliable, practical, honest Ethan: so he was known to his fellows, and so his son most easily recognized him.

"I think, sir," he began, answering his father's question, "we should take him home with us when he is able to travel. Until then..." his voice trailed off and he paused.

"Until then?" his father prompted, at last.

"Do we have an extra tunic that would fit him, and a long cloak? And he'll need a bowl, or something for water until he can use his hands to scoop with. He'll need food, too, soup, maybe; I'm not sure he can eat bread. His mouth is pretty banged up, and I'm not sure about his teeth."

"Well," began his father, but got no further.

"That's Jothan!" exploded Seth, interrupting the conversation with the suddenness of a startled hog breaking for freedom without much sense of direction. Father and son jumped, then turned to the old man.

"Oh, yes," Ethan said and shook his head sadly. "I'd forgotten he was in this area. Poor Jothan."

"Jothan," repeated Timon. "Who's Jothan? Or what's Jothan?" The boy spoke, in spite of his mother's long training on the place of children among adults and the polite silence required of them. As Seth glanced sharply at him, he closed his mouth, but his eyes looked his questions.

"Jothan," began Seth, then, looking again at Timon, he grinned suddenly and reached for his leather sack. Rummaging in it he dragged out a short tunic and tossed it at Timon. "Here, boy!" he said brusquely, "put this on! I don't want to have to answer to your mother when you come down with your death of cold! She's not that fond of my storytelling anyway, and if she finds out I was telling tales, while you were standing like a shorn lamb in the wind of them, she'll have my beard as well as my hide and no mistake!"

"Thank you, sir!" murmured Timon under his father's amused, "Now, Seth! Judith isn't that bad!" He put on the old man's tunic, which came down to his ankles, but, belted with a length of hide his father provided, did not get in his way. At Seth's command he sat and Ethan, with an expert glance at the quiet herds joined them.

"Now then!" Seth began again. "Jothan, as your father can tell you, for he was his friend, Jothan is a most unfortunate man, most unfortunate. But you cannot take him home with you like a wounded pup or a sick lamb--and not only because he wouldn't stand for it, as, in his right mind, he wouldn't. He's worse than your Judith for proper ways and pride," added Seth with a shrewd glance at Ethan, who met it without changing expression.

"Anyway," Seth continued, turning to Timon, "Jothan is dangerous. No," he held up a hand to prevent the protest he saw coming, "I know he didn't look it, or sound it today when you went to him. Did you wait for the scream?" he asked suddenly, and Timon jumped.

"Sir? The scream, sir?" Timon repeated.

Seth said, "Yes, the scream. At the end, when it comes out of him, he screams as if it were tearing out his insides from the bottom up and tearing off his fingernailes from the inside. Awful sound."

"He did scream," said Timon, "and it did sound like that--the worst kind of pain in the world. Worse, even, than Mama when Joanna came," he added to his father. Ethan nodded, but Seth looked shocked.

"You heard your mother?" he demanded.

"I was all the way down by the water, sir, but I couldn't help it," Timon said apologetically. "I knew it was Mama because Father made me stay there, and he ran back to the house. I watched where he went," he finished.

Ethan looked at Seth. "Martha is a perfectly good, ordinary midwife," he said from between clenched teeth, "but when it comes to a breech birth she should be fed to the dogs. I got there just in time."

"Have to throw her out?" inquired the older man, the edge of amusement in his voice.

"Martha? No. She took one look at me and fled." At Seth's grin he added somewhat angrily, "I didn't lay a finger on her or say a word! She just ran!"

"Surprise, surprise!" grinned Seth. Then to the mystified Timon, he explained, "Your father is the world's best assistant to any creature giving birth. The harder the birth the better he is at it, and the beasts all trust him. But the midwives think it's indecent for a husband to be anywhere around when his wife is birthing, and frankly, most men are just as glad not to be there--makes 'em feel too guilty!"

Timon looked blankly at him and said, "Sir?"

"Never mind!" said the old man hastily. "Anyway, that's why your father was down by the water with you, instead of up at the house helping Jud-your mother. And that's why Martha went flying when he did run back after your mother screamed! She knew he should have been there, and that she should have let him stay in the first place."

"Oh," said Timon. He went back to the man, Jothan it seemed his name was. "Well, sir, Jothan did scream the way you said, before he fell down. That's when I went to him."

"Then you were safe enough," said Seth. "It was out of him."

"It?" asked Timon, wrinkling his forehead. "I didn't see anything around him, and he wasn't vomiting."

"Not that kind of 'it'," said the old man impatiently. "It! The evil one! Spirits!" He finished in a whisper and glanced uneasily over his shoulder.

"Oh, sir," said Timon in a concerned tone. He reached out to pat the old man's hand in a gesture so like Ethan's that Seth blinked. "There are no spirits, you know! There is no evil one--only people who choose to be cruel to other people. You don't have to be afraid!"

Seth looked first at Timon, then at Ethan, and then back to Timon again. "Thank you, boy," he said gruffly, the sarcastic edge less in evidence in his voice than it usually was. He turned to Ethan. "You have an explanation for this, I trust?" he demanded.

"Combatting midwives foolery," said Ethan shortly. "There's enough and plenty to spare of human evil to account for all the wretchedness we're likely to run into, without having to borrow spirits to explain our cruelty away."

"You'll grant evil spirits do exist?" challenged Seth.

To Timon's surprise, Ethan paused. Then he said slowly, "Yes, they do. But they don't hide in dark corners to scare old ladies," he added looking hard at

Timon, "and they don't poison wells, kill sheep, give you cramps or steal small puppies."

Timon nodded. "But Father?" he asked, with a small shiver. "Is there such a thing as an evil spirit? And is that Jothan's 'it'?"

"Yes," said Seth, interrupting firmly, "Yes, to both questions."

"But why? How?" Timon had asked. He was badly frightened, but determined to know how his friend, for so he now thought of the injured Jothan, had gotten trapped by this shadowy force.

"That I don't know," admitted the old man. "But it's the evil spirit that attacks him all right. It started four or five years ago. Jothan'd be just fine. He was a thoroughly honest man, a banker, but one who'd help out a man if he were in trouble. Jothan never sucked blood from poor men or unlucky ones, but he was no man's fool. And he was always kind to everyone. But then--it would come on him. He'd get the wild look, and start to scream and gash himself. People were afraid. They'd chain his hands together, and his feet, and chain him to a wall, but when it was in him he could snap the chains like cord. He'd break every restraint they put on him and go running up the hill to the area of the tombs, tearing off his clothes, screaming and gashing himself with sharp rocks.

"After a time, it would leave him; you could tell by the scream when it had gone. He'd collapse for a while and then, eventually, he'd work his way back home and go to bed. Anna, his wife, would bathe him and wait on him until he recovered, and then he'd go back to work, steady as ever. Until the next time," Seth added, "and he never knew when that would be."

"I haven't seen him in years. He doesn't come back to the village now, does he?" Ethan asked. "Wasn't there something about a child?"

"His wife was carrying their first when it came on him one day," Seth replied. "He'd never have hurt her in his right mind, but when it took over, well, there was no knowing. Apparently she was trying to get out of the way when he ran at her, and she fell. He didn't stop; it drove him straight out to the hills. When Anna was able to get up she walked over to Martha's, and waited there until Martha got back from delivering twins to Jonathan's wife. By that time she was in a bad way, though. Martha tried to help her, but the child was born dead. Anna recovered, but slowly. She wasn't really well, even when Jothan came back. And when he found his wife ill, no child, and plenty of friendly folk to tell him what he had done to his wife and almost-son, that just broke his heart. The next time it came and drove him, broken chains and all, to the tombs, he stayed there. He was too ashamed to come back to his wife, though she's never blamed him a bit and really misses him."

"Excuse me, sir," said Timon softly, "but how does he live? How does he get food? Who takes care of him?"

"I'm not really sure," said Seth. "In the old days, whenever it drove him out here, his wife and his mother used to bring him food every day, and they'd put it by that big tomb with the odd shaped rock seat just left of that old tree. Then when he'd come home Anna would go and fetch the dish and the basket, and hope she'd never have to use them again. But now, I don't know."

"When did his mother die?" asked Ethan.

"Maybe two years ago," speculated Seth. "Anna's still alive--lives in their home in the west of the village near mine. It's my guess she gets food to him, but she's not well--been ailing, really, since she lost that child. I don't know how long she'll be able to keep it up."

Ethan had nodded. He looked at Timon though he addressed the swineherds in general. "I think we can get some clothes for him, son, but you'll have to take them back to him. We really can't leave the herds." To Seth he said, "From us it would be an insult. From the boy--perhaps he will accept the gift." Seth had nodded his agreement.

Timon was eager. "Yes, sir! Thank you, sir. And," he asked, "some food, and a bowl, maybe?"

No one had a bowl to spare, it seemed, but, Timon remembered, he had his own olive-wood cup. He gathered the clothing and food, thanked each of the men as he had been taught to do, then, taking his cup from its place with his father's gear, he had hurried back to where he had left Jothan.

Arriving there, he found the battered man awake and somewhat disoriented. "I've brought some clothing for you," Timon announced, "and some food." He looked at the bread and cheese doubtfully. "I hope you can eat it," he said. "I wanted soup, but there was none." He looked down at Jothan and, smiling, held out his supplies.

Jothan shook his head a bit. "Who are you?" he asked. "And why are you bringing me food and clothing?"

"I'm Timon," the boy replied to the first question, deciding, as he spoke simply to ignore the second. "I'm the son of Ethan, the shepherd. Only now," he explained parenthetically, "he has to herd swine. He can't make a living with sheep. I've brought my cup so you can have some water. Take these," he said, transferring the clothing and food to Jothan's hands, "and I'll go and get it." And off he ran.

Jothan had looked down at the bundle he was holding, shaking his head slightly. Timon? Ethan? Who were these people? For that matter, who was he? Where was he? Why was he there?

When Timon returned with the cup of water, he found Jothan as he had left him, propped awkwardly against the side of the tomb, still holding the bundle of food and clothing. "Here, let me help you," he said and put the cup down carefully. He knelt beside the battered man, removed the bundle from his hands and very gently began to dress him in the clothing the swineherds had been able to spare. It was clean and would keep him warm.

As he was shifting Jothan to adjust the full length cloak over him, he heard a murmur from the battered man. "Excuse me, sir?" he said. "I'm sorry. I didn't hear you."

"Who am I?" repeated Jothan. "And who are you?"

"I am Timon," the boy repeated. "And Seth says that you are Jothan, a banker from the village when--" he paused, "You are well."

"Jothan," repeated the man, slowly. "Jothan. I can't remember...."

"It's all right," Timon reassured him. "It doesn't matter. Drink this." He helped Jothan to drink the water he had brought from the stream, then broke off a bit of the bread and some cheese. "Try to eat this if you can," he said. "I'm going to get you more water."

Timon ran to the stream and filled the cup. On his return he found Jothan had fallen asleep. He had eaten the bread and cheese Timon had given him, and had curled up under the cloak, nestling his head into Timon's short cloak. There was almost a smile on his face. Timon placed the filled cup with the bread and cheese on a flat stone near Jothan's head. "In the morning I'll be back with more," he had said softly, and had gone back to his father and the swineherds.

From that day on, Timon had taken charge of Jothan's survival. He found Jothan's house and spoke to his wife, Anna, who was touched by the boy's concern for Jothan and grateful for his help. She gave him fresh clothing for Jothan, as well as soap and towels, in case Jothan should wish them, but these Timon hid by the tomb. Jothan seemed disinclined to bathe and apparently preferred to run naked even in the coldest weather. Anna also provided soup and bread for her husband when she was able to cook. She gave Timon two of Jothan's striped bowls and two of the three-sectioned baskets she had woven for him. These he used to carry food to Jothan every day. Timon's grandmother, when she drew from Timon an admission of where he was going so early every day, also provided bread and soup for the beleaguered man.

Sometimes when he brought provisions, Timon saw Jothan. Three times they were able to speak, and two other times Jothan had recognized Timon in the distance and had waved to him but had run away as Timon approached. Mostly, though, Timon had just found the empty containers, replaced them with full ones and, having checked the hidden stores, had gone quietly back the way he had come.

Now, almost a year later, Timon sat watching Jothan, noting the clutching movements of his hands and the odd rigidity of his collapse. He had thought Jothan was just coming out of an attack and was hoping to speak to him, but now it seemed he was not.

As Timon watched, Jothan suddenly stiffened and was raised to his feet. It did not seem to Timon that he got up; rather he was hoisted up and dropped on his feet. His head went back, his eyes were slitted almost shut, and his lips were pulled back in the parody of a grin that expressed more pain than a scream. He turned in place until he was pointed at the path to the village, and then, stiffly, he moved along that path, not seeming to see where he was going, yet never stumbling, even when rocks rolled out from under his feet.

Concerned, Timon rose from his place and prepared to follow Jothan. What he could do he did not know, but he wanted to be there in case he could help, or in case Jothan should come to himself and be frightened.

Jothan made his way swiftly along the path, hurrying as if he had a reason to get to the village, an appointment to keep, a job to do, and had to be there by a certain time. Timon had to hurry to keep him in sight. The path ran, for a time, beside the fields where the hogs were feeding. Timon caught sight of Seth and waved to him but signalled him to keep silent, pointing to Jothan some way ahead of him. Seth took in the situation at a glance, nodded once to Timon and went to find Ethan to tell him what was happening. He had seen that Timon was staying at a prudent distance from the galvanized, abstracted Jothan, and knew the boy would be safe as long as he kept his head and left a clear path behind him. Seth was concerned, but not worried, and he admired young Timon as much for his kind heart and silent self-sacrifice as for his courage and ingenuity. Ethan had a good firstborn son there; would that Jothan had had the same! "Perhaps he does," Ethan had suggested when Seth had said as much to him. "Certainly if Timon's choosing has any weight, Jothan will always have a father's honor. It's one of the things about Timon that makes me proud to have sired him." Seth had often pondered that remark as he did now.

Meanwhile, out of Seth's sight, Jothan started down the hill, the last stretch of road leading to the village. Timon, taking what cover he could find, moved closer. If Jothan needed help, it would be now that they were approaching a more peopled area.

Suddenly Jothan stopped short. He swiveled slightly on his heels, first turning to the right and then to the left as if seeking the exact direction he was to take. Then, aimed, he poised for an instant, rocked for-ward onto his toes, emitted a scream of pain, rage and mis-ery that turned heads, drew people into the street and stood Timon's hair on end, and began to run headlong down the hill. He was not following the path. Indeed, he seemed to blaze a path of his own, so swiftly did he run. The unearthly scream continued as he ran. Timon, close behind him now and not troubling to seek cover, could not understand how that scream could just go on and on. Jothan did not break the blade of sound, though, like Timon, he was gasping for air at the exertion of the run. Timon could see his chest heaving and even hear the rasp of air as Jothan panted, but the scream swelled unbroken, intensifying in volume as it rose in pitch.

It was then that Timon understood the fact of the demon's possession of Jothan, and saw the suffering of the human shell which the evil power had chosen for its vessel. He began to shiver, and felt a scream of his own rising in his chest and throat to match the eerie shriek pouring from Jothan.

But even as Timon strove to press back the scream, Jothan was stopped short by the force within him and flung to the ground, physically all but spent, at the feet of a man who was partly surrounded by a crowd of people, partly villagers and partly strangers. The scream stopped as suddenly as it had begun and words began. The voice which shouted them was both Jothan's and not Jothan's. It was the evil spirit, Timon knew, and he felt his scalp prickle.

"Why meddle with me, Jesus, Son of God," shouted the voice the demon was taking from Jothan. The tone was arrogant, hostile and, in a strange way, cringing. Timon wondered why. He looked at the man at whose feet the demon had flung Jothan. Why should the demon fear this ordinary-looking, poor man with the kind, aware eyes and firm mouth? Timon himself wanted very much, though he could not say why, to explain to the man that, really, Jothan meant no harm, and that he was not responsible for what was coming out of his mouth. He was about to say, "Sir? Jesus?" when he realized that the man Jesus had locked eyes with was Jothan, and that he was speaking to Jothan, or rather to the demon within him.

"Come out of the man, unclean spirit!" commanded Jesus, quietly, and Jothan's body began to writhe.

"I implore you in God's name, do not torture me!" whined the demon through Jothan's twisted lips. The tone was as servile as it was filled with hatred. There was no mistaking it, thought Timon. This Jesus was the demon's master, and both he and the demon knew it. Timon moved so that he could see Jothan's eyes. Perhaps it would help Jothan not to be afraid if he could see a familiar face--if he was able to recognize Timon, of course.

But when he was able to look into Jothan's eyes, he had a shock. Jothan's eyes were still held in Jesus' steady gaze, but they were full of peace. The tears Jothan was weeping were tears of relief and gratitude. Part, at least, of Jothan was free from the demon's tyranny, and he was clinging with all the strength he could muster to Jesus who had engaged the demon (and so, partly, freed him).

Timon backed away then, content that the battle being won would be more effectively concluded without his interference. He would simply wait and be ready to help, when and if he should be needed.

"What is your name?" The quiet question which Jesus spoke was really the command of the victor to the vanquished, and both Jothan, to his joy, and the demon, to his torment, recognized it as an unrefusable demand.

"Legion is my name," the demon replied through Jothan. "There are hundreds of us."

Poor Jothan, Timon thought, compassion washing over him in a flood-tide. How dreadful to have been held captive by so many foul spirits for all this time! He wished he could hug Jothan or comfort him for his past pain, but, looking at him, gratitude brimming from the eyes he had fastened on Jesus, Timon knew his sympathy was not, now, needed.

The demon was still speaking, using Jothan's body to grovel and fawn upon Jesus. Legion was begging for something not entirely clear to Timon, gabbling about not being sent out of the area or not being sent back into the abyss. Finally a concrete proposal emerged from between Jothan's bared teeth with the distorted grimace the demon meant for a placating smile. "Send us into the herd of swine," Legion pleaded.

Timon looked up. There was the herd, about two thousand swine, peacefully feeding on the side of the hill he and Jothan had just careened down. He could not see Seth nor his father nor the other herdsmen, but he knew they were there. They would not be pleased if Jesus granted Legion's request, though they would be glad for Jothan's sake. But the owners of the hogs would be furious, and the herdsmen might suffer. Suppose the hogs started screaming as Jothan did, or refused to eat?

But Jesus was nodding reflectively. "Go," He said and, with the tearing scream with which they were accustomed to depart from Jothan, the demons left him in an exhausted heap at Jesus' feet where he reached out to touch his healer and fainted.

The demons apparently went directly from Jothan into the hogs, for with a concerted howling snort the whole two thousand stood stiff-legged and rigid, wheeled in a single motion and thundered past them straight down the bluff and into the lake where they began to drown.

On their heels came the swineherds, though the men kept to the path. Seeing the fate of their charges and being unable either to prevent it or to rescue the drowning hogs, they ran on to the fields and the village to tell everyone what happened. Timon saw Ethan and Seth among the herders, but neither had eyes for him.

When the dust had settled, Timon saw Jesus looking down at the still unconscious Jothan. He bent over him and Jothan, reviving, began to thank Jesus. He was fully in possession of himself, Timon saw with relief, and was supremely happy.

Suddenly Jothan stopped speaking. A look of horror spread from his eyes to his mouth. He raised his hands to cover his reddening face, then dropped them, then raised them again, trying, it seemed, to disappear altogether. What on earth was wrong with him? Had the legion or some fraction of it returned?

Timon, alarmed, came forward swiftly to see what he could do, if anything. He looked at the writhing Jothan for a moment, and then, suddenly, he understood what Seth had said to Ethan about Jothan that first day he had seen the possessed man--"worse than your Judith for proper ways and pride." Now that Legion was gone, Jothan knew he was stark naked, and he was ashamed. Whipping off his own cloak Timon covered Jothan with it. "It's all right, sir," he said to the exhausted Jothan. "Come with me. I have clothes for you up at the tomb. And your wife sent you some soap and towels so you can bathe in the stream if you want to. I'm Timon," he added, not knowing if Jothan would remember him. "I'm just your friend."

"Thank you, Timon," said Jothan, wrapping the cloak around him securely. "I know you well."

The boy and the man turned to Jesus to explain, but found that no explanation was necesary. "We'll come up to that big tomb by the tree when we're finished," said Timon, and Jesus smiling, nodded and began to gather his own followers from among the villagers who fell back quietly and trailed Jesus' group up the hill.

When Jothan had bathed and dressed, with Timon's tactful assistance, he went back up the rise to the tomb which had served as his home for several years, without his having been aware of it. There he found Jesus waiting for him and, going quietly to Him, sat at His feet, the traditional position of the disciple in the presence of his master.

On Jothan's face was such joy and longing that Timon backed away. He wanted to know more of this Jesus who had saved his friend, but he knew better than to intrude here. Obviously Jesus and Jothan would have much to say to each other, and now that Jothan was fully himself again, he would need some privacy to be able to express himself to Jesus, as he so plainly wanted and needed to do.

As Timon backed away, the movement attracted Jesus' attention and He threw the boy a single glance so full of love, understanding, gratitude and approval that Timon, who had caught the look full force, gasped slightly. He felt himself filled to the brim with a joy whose name he would only later learn was rapture, a joy that set his soul singing and left him so utterly content, so fulfilled that he had nothing further to wish. Humming a small tune he did not know he knew, Timon moved well out of earshot of the two at the tomb and took up watch at the head of the path up which the rest of the villagers would have to come if they wanted to find Jesus.

And they did want to find Him, though not for Jothan's reasons. It was the two thousand drowned swine that had most of them in an uproar, and had them frightened as well. Ethan and Seth, recognized spokesmen for the herders had been graphic in their description of the effects of Legion upon their charges.

They hadn't been too clear about where this magical force, for so they saw it, had come from, but they knew, and the other herdsmen corroborated their testimony, that it had something to do with the Galilean who had just come ashore with his followers, and had been climbing the path leading to the uplands beyond the village with them and some idle villagers when Jothan, "worse than ever," had met him. Suddenly, off the hogs had run, straight into the lake, all two thousand of them!

The owners of the hogs and the rest of the villagers decided that they'd better "see about all this" and, driven by this odd mix of anger and fear, with Ethan and Seth in the lead, they headed for the path on which Timon stood as unofficial sentry.

"Father!" the boy caroled joyfully, as his father and Seth came into view. "Good day, sir," he greeted Seth, then rushed on, "Father! Jothan is well again! Jesus drove out the evil spirits and let them go into the hogs. It said its name was Legion when Jesus asked," he added, turning to Seth. "You were right sir; it was an evil spirit all right--hundreds of them, Legion said."

"Evil spirits are liars," Ethan reminded him.

"There are no hogs left up here, are there?" asked Seth, innocently.

"No," said Ethan, then looked sharply at Seth who gazed pointedly around the field. "All right," he said, after a pause, "Legion. Now, Timon, where is Jothan, did you say? And where is this Jesus?"

"Over there, sir," replied his son and turned to lead the way.

Behind Seth and Ethan a large number of townsfolk had come up. One of them asked in general, "Does anyone know where this Jesus is who destroyed all our hogs?"

"He's over here, sir," Timon answered, "but He didn't destroy the hogs. Legion did."

"Who is Legion?" asked another portly man who had shoved his way through the crowd and now stood, puffing and swelling importantly, between the crowd and Ethan, Seth and Timon.

"Legion is the devil, or the group of evil spirits, that have been tormenting Jothan for so long." It was Ethan who answered. Seth looked at him with some surprise, but said nothing.

"Well, how did Legion get out of Jothan and into my hogs?" demanded the portly man.

"That was Jesus! He healed Jothan!" Timon broke in, too excited to realize that the portly man cared not at all for Jothan and his troubles; he was interested only in his hogs. "Isn't it wonderful sir?" he finished, beaming up at the man.

"Jesus took Legion out of Jothan and put him in my hogs?" The portly man's anger had become quiet but dangerous; Timon missed the signal and, tumbling over himself in his enthusiasm, assured the questioner that Jesus had taken Legion out of Jothan but hadn't actually put him into the hogs; Legion had asked to go into them, and Jesus had agreed. Then Legion had left Jothan, "and now he's just fine, sir! Isn't that wonderful?"

"No," said the portly man flatly. "No. Its not wonderful, not wonderful at all, and you're a young fool if you think it is. Do you know how much those hogs were worth? Do you have any idea how much money Jothan, and this Legion, and your precious Jesus have cost me today? Where is he? Someone's going to pay for this! Where is this Jesus? Never mind," he finished, pushing Timon roughly aside so that the boy almost fell. "I see him. You there!" he shouted, striding over toward Jesus, where Jothan, fully clothed and in possession of his faculties, was sitting with Jesus.

"What? What's the problem Simeon? What are you sputtering about!" The speaker was Jothan. He rose and faced the mob, which fell back to a respectful distance before his firm authority, leaving Simeon to his fate.

The portly man was startled, and somewhat abashed, for he had never thought to see Jothan in his old form. The thought of the two thousand lost hogs, of which seven hundred fifty had been his, gave him a kind of courage, though, and he squared up to Jothan with a bravado he did not entirely feel. "I've lost all my hogs and it's your fault. Or somebody's," he said, not quite looking at Jesus. "I want something done!"

"What?" asked Jothan coldly. "And by whom?"

"Well," sputtered Simeon, "I want...I think...you... he has to get out of here. You must leave us," he said directly to Jesus, and then, in spite of himself added, "please, sir!"

There was a placatory murmur from the crowd seconding Simeon's demand which had so swiftly become a request. "Please, sir," said another voice, "would you mind very much going away?"

"Vermin!" hissed Jothan. "You scum, Andras!" He drew a deep breath, preparatory to flaying the speaker with a few well-chosen sentences, when he felt the hand of Jesus on his own. "Master?" he asked. Jesus shook His head. "I shall go," He said quietly to Jothan, whose face fell.

"But Master!" he protested. "I can deal with this set of nothings with no trouble at all. They'll settle down at once. All they need is a firm hand!"

Jesus shook his head, smiling. "That is not My way," He said simply. Then He signalled, and his companions gathered inquiringly around Him. "We are going now," He informed them and headed back down the path He had climbed, with them trailing obediently behind Him.

Jothan and Timon exchanged glances. "But," said Jothan, and ran after Jesus. "Master?" he said as he came up to Jesus. He knelt at Jesus' feet. "Take me with you, please?" he begged. "If they won't have You, I don't want to live here. Let me go with You wherever You go! Let me be one of Your followers!"

Timon heard the last words of the speech as he caught up to Jothan. He was standing to one side of the healed banker and so could see both Jothan and Jesus as the Master replied, regretfully, it seemed to the boy, but with a certainty that matched Jothan's own. "No,"

He said. "You may not come with us." At Jothan's
disappointed face, and the naked plea in his eyes, Jesus
smiled and placed His hand on Jothan's head. "Go,"
He said, "go home to your family, and make it clear to
them how much the Lord, in His mercy, has done for
you."

Jothan stared into Jesus' eyes for a long minute of
silence. Then as he rose to his feet, he too began to
smile, though Timon who had come to know him better
than anyone else in the town, except Anna, could see a
suspicion of tears in his eyes and hear them in his
voice as he said, "Yes, Master." Timon stepped forward quickly and grasped Jothan's hand in his own,
looking up at him. The man looked down quickly at
the boy, met his eyes for a single instant and bit his
lips. Then, returning the pressure of Timon's hand,
he straightened himself proudly. "It shall be as you
will, my Lord," he announced, his voice carrying the
pain and joy of a well-blown war-trumpet. "We shall
tell everyone!"

Jesus smiled, touching man and boy in that single
glance with a love that neither had known before, and
each would remember until death summoned him
home. Then, turning, He walked toward the boat.

When the group had shoved the boat away from the
shore and the rowers had carried it out of sight, Jothan
looked down at Timon who returned the look with a
smile of sheer joy. "Timon," he began, and then
paused. "Son, we have much work to do," he said
finally, "Let us go to your father--"

"I'm right here, Jothan," said Ethan quietly. "It
seems to me my son is yours now as well, and you two
have been given work to do. It will be easier for you to
obey the Master if Timon stays in your house--unless
you find him troublesome. He is a good lad and will
give you his best service, I am sure," Ethan finished.
He shot Timon an inscrutable look, but the lad only
grinned at his father. "I shall endeavor to please you
in all you command, my father," he responded formally, bowing to Ethan. Then he beamed again at his

father. "Thank you sir," he all but sang. "Oh, thank you, father!"

The smile that lit Timon's face was reflected in Ethan's eyes, though the older man's expression remained unreadable. He looked at Jothan. "Does this please you, my friend?" he asked. "Will my son be acceptable to you as a member of your household"?

Jothan gazed back at Ethan. He opened his mouth to speak but found no words and so closed it again. He cleared his throat, blinked rapidly three times and then said, "Most acceptable indeed, my good friend, both because he is your son and because, in this endless year, he has chosen to be mine, and my faithful friend as well. God has blessed you indeed to have given you such a son, and you have returned the blessing with praise by the man you have made of him. I thank you for this gift, but God will reward you for it!" Then to Timon who was still holding his hand Jothan said, "Well, lad? We must take these things home to Ann--to your second mother. She will be wondering what kept us!"

"Yes, sir," replied Timon. He let go of Jothan for an instant to hug Ethan. "Tell Grandmother and Mama," he began, but Ethan cut him short.

"They know, I think, or will be able to guess, but I shall give them and your brothers and sisters your love," he answered Timon. "Now, on your way! Jothan is waiting."

Timon nodded. "Yes sir!" he said. "Thank you, father!" He smiled all the joy in his heart at Ethan, then turned to Jothan, extending his hand. "Sir?" he said.

Jothan took Timon's hand in his own. "To the tomb first," he said, "to pick up all our gear. And then," he smiled at Timon who beamed back at him, "then, home!" They strode up the path together as Ethan watched, smiling, then turned to follow the track Seth had taken toward the village. He, too, was going home.

Jairus

There was only one thing in the mind of Jairus this warm morning as he hurried from his home toward the Capernaum shore of the Sea of Galilee. His daughter, his only child, was dying. She was twelve years old.

Just a week ago last Thursday the whole family had celebrated the event--and now she was dying. Her vivid coloring had faded, her lively dark eyes had grown dull, her hair had become lusterless and brittle and her flesh had seemed to melt from her frame, leaving the delicate bones all but visible as she tossed and turned in the grip of the fever which had claimed her a week--no, longer--nine days ago and now seemed about to swallow her life.

"No! She shall not die!" The words Jairus grated out came from between his gritted teeth with the force of that fury which only deadly fear evokes. With a clenched fist he pounded an invisible table. "She must not die! God! She must not die! You are the only God, the Lord of Life. You gave her to me. You must not take her back! You gave Abraham his only son when you had commanded Isaac's death and his grieving father's dagger was making its downward arc over Isaac's bound body laid on your altar. You gave him back his child in Your mercy. Give me mine! God! Give me back my only, my most beautiful child!"

This was not Jairus' usual style of prayer, as the haste with which he moved toward Capernaum was not his customary traveling pace. Indeed, the leader of the synagogue was known for his deliberateness of speech and action. In times of crisis or of deep emotion he spoke after longer reflection, even more slowly and softly, and with longer pauses between phrases. He was a man of God, always aware of the presence of God as Israel's true Center, and always quietly in search of His will. For Jairus, the keeping of the Law was a labor of love, and he lavished on the details of observance the joyous attentive fidelity another man might pour out upon his wife, his children or his business.

And Jairus loved his family as well as his God and the community of Israel. He worked hard to provide a comfortable home for his wife, her mother, his father, Aunt Leah and his beloved daughter, Rachel, and his delight in all of them was repaid by their care for him, and their mild rivalry in supplying the things he particularly enjoyed.

In his home, in his shop, where he was a sandal-maker by trade, and in the synagogue, wherever Jairus presided, all was order, all was calm. He could not bear it to be otherwise, and no one around him could bear to disappoint him.

His haste this day, like his frantic prayer, would have startled and frightened his daughter, had she seen and heard him, for never in her experience of him had Rachel known her father to be anything but measured, calm, gentle, and in complete command of himself and of his world.

Jairus himself recognized the frantic quality of his thoughts and actions, recognized and accepted both the source and the results of this anarchic passion let loose in him to wreak havoc. He did not care. He would save his daughter, whatever it took, and if he could not....

Moving even faster, Jairus tried to banish the very possibility of a failure by recalling every detail of his daughter's existence as vividly as if his memory of her, living, could keep the threatened life from flowing out of her as the fever ate its way through her substance.

Her birth had brought a joy to Jairus and his wife Rebecca that they had not known before. The child was beautiful from the start. Where most infants are red, rubbery and somewhat alien creatures of insatiable appetite and insistent, entirely self-centered demands, Rachel had been quiet and content. She seemed to recognize the atmosphere of orderly peace and quiet love that Jairus evoked wherever he was, and to respond to it with gurgling good cheer, as her mother always had.

Like Rebecca, Rachel was a small-boned, pale-skinned, dark-haired beauty. She had her father's large, dark eyes, but where his were still, reflective pools, hers sparkled with her mother's quick laughter, or snapped with Rebecca's hot temper. But in the daughter as in the mother, the temper flare-ups were few and quickly, completely over, once the explosion was finished, and joy was dominant again.

It was Jairus' father who had given Rachel the name she preferred and the family members always used. When he saw her in her proud father's arms he smiled wonderingly. Extending an index finger to her, he said to her, "Talitha! Will you be my little girl, my Talitha?" and the child, seeming to understand the grave old man who smiled with his eyes and his voice though not often with his mouth, had grasped his finger and crowed joyfully.

From that point on, Grandfather Jacob would only call the child Talitha, and the rest of the family, one by one, adopted the name. By the time she could say their names and her own, young Rachel thought of herself as "really Talitha, though outside the family people call me Rachel." Even now, at her twelfth birthday festival, the last she would have as a child, everyone called her Talitha.

Privately her mother wondered about the persistence of the nickname and her daughter's unusual affection for it, when her friends and cousins, some younger than she, were all struggling to break their ties to their childhood and to discard all the things that made them "babies." These youngsters were racing as fast as they were allowed to travel toward adulthood, while her daughter seemed not only content, but determined, to remain a child indefinitely.

Rebecca had wondered whether the almost-grown-up gifts Rachel received at the party might not wake her up to reality of her approaching womanhood, and had hoped that it might be so. She did not voice either the question or the hope to her father-in-law, who seemed as content as Rachel that she should go on being "his Talitha" but to Jairus she had said, "The silver bracelets of your mother, I think, must go to Rachel this year. They were your father's wedding gift to his bride, and it is time that Rachel began to think of her own wedding. It's only a couple of years away, and she must begin to accustom herself to the idea of being a woman, a wife and a mother."

"But," Jairus had objected, "Talitha is only going to be twelve!"

"I was thirteen when you married me," Rebecca had reminded him.

Jairus was silent for several long minutes. Then he said quietly and judiciously, "Talitha-Rachel is not like you in that. But you are right. It is time for her to have the bracelets and to begin to turn toward her future. We must begin to call her Rachel, too, but not all at once. Too abrupt a transition could damage her, I think. Once a day at first, perhaps, and then, gradually more often..." His voice had trailed off, as he retreated into thought, and neither parent had again raised the subject. But Talitha had gotten her grandmother's silver wedding bracelets for her birthday, and every day her father had addressed her, at least once, as Rachel.

What the child had made of it all Jairus did not know. Rachel knew the story of her grandmother's wedding bracelets, of course, and knew also that they would be hers when she was old enough to marry. She loved their smooth curves and had often handled them admiringly while she was growing up. But when they appeared at the center of the table of gifts, she had not exclaimed over them nor asked about them. All she had done was to run an index finger around the rim of each and then turn with a questioning glance to her grandfather.

The old man had not seen her turn nor felt her eyes on him, for when he saw the bracelets sitting on the table he had gone back in time to the day nearly forty years earlier when he had presented them to Anna, the bride who had caught his heart, and even now, thirty

years after her death still held it in the palm of her
hand. Anna had smiled at him that day, with all the
love of her heart, and, deep in his memory of that love,
old Jacob smiled back at his Anna and nodded slightly.
And so his grandaughter, seeing the smile and thinking it was meant for her, had turned back to the table.
In her eyes there was pain, but she put on the bracelets
carefully. If this was what her grandfather wanted of
her, she would be "his Talitha;" she would obey.

Jairus, remembering the scene he had observed, at
the time uncomprehendingly, suddenly understood it.
The communication between his father and his daughter, up to this point almost uncanny in its completeness, had been, in this single instance, completely
broken without either of them realizing it, so that each
might thereafter be free and neither might wholly lose
the other. Rachel thought her grandfather's smile and
nod had told her to put on her grandmother's bracelets
and to begin to take upon herself the burdens and
glories, equally unknown, of her own womanhood.
And Jacob, had seen "his" Talitha turn to the table,
take up the bracelets that had been Anna's, put them
on and turn to him and smile with what seemed to be
satisfaction at her new almost-grown status.

As he hurried on his way to the shore Jairus
realized that he was the only one who knew that
Talitha had put on her bracelets and her coming
womanhood with a brave smile for Jacob because she
thought that that was what her beloved grandfather
desired of her, and that Jacob had smiled bravely in
return because he thought Rachel had wanted to leave
her childhood, her place as "his Talitha," and he would
not stand in her way. Jairus shook his head ruefully.
Even, perhaps especially, for people who loved each
other, life was a complicated, painful business.

It was almost at this point that the hurrying
synagogue leader met and almost collided with Sarah,
a widow some ten years younger than Jacob. As a
child Jairus had stayed with her and her husband
when his mother was ill, and when she had died,

Sarah had comforted the lad and given him an unofficial second home. Her own husband had died at about the time Jairus had married his beloved Rebecca, and, though her husband's kin made her welcome, and she had gone to dwell, in their homes, it was with Jairus and Rebecca that Sarah felt most comfortable. She would visit from time to time, staying with them as she pursued her so far fruitless search for someone who would cure her.

Several years ago Sarah had explained to Rebecca (who had, of course, told Jairus as Sarah had meant she should), that she had been suffering from a mysterious hemorrhage that had started at about the time Rachel was born, and that, though she had spent all the money her husband had left her on various remedies and doctors, none of the medical men had been able to find the cause of her affliction and none of their cures had worked.

Encountering her now, Jairus was startled. He had last seen her six months earlier, and she had said then that she was feeling better. She was hopeful that her new doctor would find the cure that had eluded the others. Now, even as he inquired, "Sarah! How are you?" Jairus was thinking how thin and drawn she looked. The dark circles under her eyes seemed to have been carved into her face, while the bone structure was almost as visible as that of his dying Rachel.

"Not well, Jairus, not well," she responded, and then, characteristically turned the focus of the conversation to her questioner's interests. "How is your family?" she asked. "Jacob? Rebecca? Rachel? Leah? Jairus, what's wrong? What's happened?"

Jairus had been about to answer Sarah's first question noncommittally, but as he heard her voice lovingly caress the names of those dearest to him, the tears that had been rising in him since the start of Rachel's illness spilled over, and in spite of himself, in defiance of a lifetime's habit of discretion and careful control, the leader of the synagogue stood in the street and wept aloud like an abandoned five-year old.

Sarah swept him into her familiar motherly embrace and simply held him until the storm had spent itself. Then she dried his eyes with her cloak, kissed him gently and quietly repeated, "What's wrong, son? What has happened?"

"Rachel is dying and no one knows why," replied Jairus, his voice growing steadier as he spoke. "She came down with a fever nine days ago, just after her twelfth birthday, and nothing we've done, or the doctors have advised, has reduced it. It has simply eaten her up. She's nothing but skin and bones. They say she won't live the night, and I believe them."

"Doctors! Much good they are!" snorted Sarah. "You must get to Jesus the prophet," she continued vigorously. "If anyone can heal her he can. He should be getting back today from the Geresene territory. At least that's what I was told by the people who claim to know. Come with me! I'm going down to where they usually dock their boats. Maybe they can tell us there."

"I'm glad I met you, Sarah," said Jairus simply. "That's why I've come into town, to find Jesus and bring him back home with me. Which way do we go?"

"Over here," responded the old woman, and headed to her left so promptly that it did not occur to Jairus to ask her where she had been going nor why. He simply assumed that her only purpose was to get him to Jesus, and, as he followed her, he retreated again into his deepening fog of anxiety and anger.

For her part, Sarah was content that he should do so. Her concerns could wait in this emergency; indeed, she was glad rather than otherwise, to be forgotten this morning of all the days in the world, for what she intended to do could be done only if she did not state it, even to herself, much less to anyone as practical and reasonable as her "son" Jairus usually was. It was a piece of luck, she reflected, that he was so preoccupied with his own troubles this morning, or perhaps...?

Hurrying ahead of him toward the waterfront from which the confused murmur of a huge crowd could already be heard, Sarah dropped her thought in mid-sentence. That track would do no one good. She tugged at Jairus's sleeve. "When we get to the waterfront," she said, "look to your left. The fourth boat down the line is the one he uses, and he and his friends will probably still be in the vicinity. From the sound of things, the crowds have jammed the streets again, so he won't have been able to get away. If we split up, we'll have a better chance of getting to him. Whoever gets to him first will ask him to go to see Rachel. All right?"

"Sarah, you're wonderful!" exclaimed Jairus. "But what does he look like? How will I know him?"

"He'll be where the crowd's the thickest, at the center of it," replied Sarah. "You'll probably see Simon, Jonah's son--the fisherman--before you spot Jesus. Simon is simply huge, and he sticks closer to Jesus than a man's shadow at noon."

"I know Jonah well, and I've seem Simon often enough, though I've not spoken to him, and I didn't know he had joined Jesus' group. You're right--he'll make a good landmark! Sarah, thank you," he added as the old woman was about to leave him.

She smiled. "We must get him to go to our Rachel-- that's what matters," she said and, hurrying around the corner, plunged into the crowd.

Jairus, noting the direction she had taken, moved into the street opposite and found himself caught up into the crowd. He was able to spot the mast of "the fourth boat down" just before the crew took it down, and pointing himself in that direction began to make what progress he could.

He soon found himself wedged in, his way forward blocked by a stout merchant and his wife, and his side exits cut off, on the left by three members of the synagogue in heated argument, and on the right by some folk in from the country who had stopped, in a knot, as bewildered by the deafening crowd roar and milling confusion as one of their cows would have been.

And then the desperation took over. "Let me through!" he commanded his fellow synagogue members in a tone a Roman legionaire might have

envied for its authoritative force. Obediently, the
debators made a small space for him and Jairus, using
elbows, hands and knees and feet in ways he did not
know he knew, forced a passage way through the
throng, oblivious to the startled looks and angry voices
he left in his wake. He was going to get to Jesus, now,
if he had to walk on heads and grind reverend beards
into the dirt of the roadway to do it.

Sarah, working her way into the crowd's center saw
Jesus jammed up against the house wall where the
crowd had pushed him. She could also see the evidence
of Jairus' progress as he neared his goal, and in spite
of her double anxiety, for the dying Rachel and for
herself, she smiled, shaking her head a bit. "If anyone
had told me five years ago that I'd live to see Jairus of
Capernaum pick up a servant of the High Priest by the
scruff of his neck and the back of his tunic and simply
move him out of his path like the loathsome toad he is,"
she murmured, but just then Jairus catapaulted
through the last layer of the crowd, landing on his
knees at Jesus' feet. At once he bowed, face to the
ground.

Then, clutching Jesus around the knees he pleaded
in a voice that cut through the crowd noise like a silver
knife through soft cheese, or like the ram's horn
signalling the start of the festival to the excited crowds
in Jerusalem. "My twelve year-old daughter is dying.
Please, sir, come home with me and lay your hands on
her so that she may get well and live."

Jesus, looking into the eyes of the synagogue leader,
mirrored in his own the pain he found there. He nodded and reached down to help Jairus rise. Jairus, once
risen, kept his right hand firmly around Jesus' left
wrist so that the crowds might not separate them. He
turned, and pulling Jesus after him began to move in
the direction from which he had come, forcing a way
for the two of them with his newly discovered skill at
making an opening where one could not possibly exit.

Sighing with relief, for she knew that once Jesus
touched Rachel the child would be healed, Sarah re-

turned to her own preoccupation. When Jairus had all but run her down, she had been seeking Jesus herself. She had intended to ask him to cure her of the hemorrhage which had been growing steadily worse.

Now, though she had not changed her objective, and continued to follow Jesus as Jairus led him away, she reconsidered her plan. Obviously, Jesus must not be delayed in getting to Rachel. The child must be very near death to have driven Jairus so far from his accustomed habits and attitudes. But if she could manage to get close enough to Jesus to touch him, she would be healed. He wouldn't have to stop, would never even have to know. Once she made contact with the healing power that emanated from him, all would be well.

As she struggled forward, Sarah noticed that the cloak Jesus wore was being pulled back from his shoulder by the pressure of the crowd. In fact, she could almost touch the tassel at the corner of it, though she was still a man's length away from him. She reached forward, shoved firmly against the solid bulk of a local vendor of pastries and with her left thumb and first two fingers she snatched at the elusive tassel. Twice she missed it, but the third time caught and held it firmly for an instant, before the movement of the crowd, like a great wave, pushed between them and pulled the tassel from her grip.

But it had been enough. Two things happened simultaneously. Sarah felt the hemorrhage within her dry up at its source. She was entirely, completely and permanently healed at last--of that she had no doubt. And Jesus had done it, though she had said nothing to him, and he did not even know she existed.

The second thing that happened was that Jesus stopped moving. "Who touched me?" he demanded, and, in spite of the frantic tugging of Jairus on his left wrist, stood where he was, looking all around him.

Amid the chorus of "Not me!" and "What does he mean?" Simon Peter, "Rock" indeed of the core of his followers as Jesus had so aptly nicknamed him, looked at the Master startled. "Lord?" he asked. "What do you mean 'who touched me?' Everybody's touching you! We're so jammed in here a man can't raise his hand to scratch his nose without putting an elbow in his neighbor's eye! I've probably stepped on you once or twice myself, though I certainly didn't mean to!"

But Jesus brushed aside the elaboration like a bothersome fly. "Somebody touched me," he insisted. "I know that power has gone forth from me." He continued to search the crowds, ignoring all anyone could say about the impossibility of finding any one person who had touched him differently from the rest, and ignoring too the frantic Jairus, attached to his left wrist and all but gibbering in his frustration at this unscheduled halt.

Finally, Simon Peter, shrugging his shoulders lapsed into silence. There was nothing he or anyone else could do. They would have to wait until whoever it was came forward, or, failing that, until Jesus gave up the search. It looked like a long morning.

At that point Sarah wriggled through the crowd and knelt at Jesus' feet, trembling, with the combination of ecstatic joy at her deliverance, concern for Rachel whom her independent, secret act had, apparently, jeopardized by stopping Jesus on his already slowed way to heal her, and fear lest he be angry with her for taking from him what she had not been able to ask him for. She had meant only to help Jairus and Rachel by not delaying him, but suppose he thought she was just too arrogant to beg for God's gifts, and so selfish that she thought she had a right to anything she saw and had the wit and nerve to snatch? She would have to explain.

"It was I who touched you, sir," she began and her voice was firm as she described her illness and all she had done these past twelve years to obtain a cure, to no avail. "Sir, since I knew if I touched even the tassel of your cloak I'd be healed, and since I didn't want to stop you on your way to heal Jairus' daugther," she finished, "I caught hold of that tassel," and she touched it again with her index finger. Meeting his eyes with the candor of a child she said, "At that very moment I was completely cured--just then, when I caught hold of this tassel of your cloak!"

Jesus smiled at her. "Daughter," he said gently, "it is your faith that has cured you." He touched her head lightly with his free right hand then helped her to rise. "Now go in peace, and remain free of this illness," he said and smiled again.

Jairus, who had, for the length of this exchange, fallen silent in spite of himself, now began to tug at Jesus' left wrist again. "Please, sir," he begged. "Please sir! We must hurry! Please, sir, come with me."

As Jesus turned from Sarah to meet Jairus' eyes and pleading voice with restored attention, another voice cut through the general racket which had risen significantly. News of Sarah's cure was spreading through the pressing crowd from the center to the edges as the motion of a stone dropped in the center of a lake is communicated to its edges, and as it travelled the noise level increased. But this voice cut through the waves of sound with a contemptuous edge that roused Jairus to rage, even as the message dropped upon his desperate hopes like an enormous rock. "Jairus," drawled the voice insolently, "your daughter is dead. Don't bother the teacher any further."

The blood drained from Jairus' face as the import of what the speaker had said penetrated. Benjamin, an unsuccessful rival of Jairus for leadership in the synagogue, had been bitter ever since the ascendency of the sandal-maker had been established, and had never missed an opportunity to make a cruel remark, but he was no liar. One glance confirmed Jairus' fears. Benjamin was telling the truth, however maliciously. Rachel was dead. They were too late.

Jairus released Jesus' wrist and drooped. Hopeless tears welled up in his eyes and began to trace slow paths down his dusty cheeks. They were too late. He had failed. His daughter was dead. It was too late.

Too late.

And then he became aware that Jesus was still looking at him, talking to him. He sorted out the words into a sentence. Jesus had said, was saying, "Fear is useless. What is needed is trust." Then catching hold of Jairus' now limp right hand with his left and giving it a quick squeeze, he locked the synagogue leader's right wrist in a reassuring grip, and added, "Only trust, and her life will be saved."

Jairus could not have said how they got from the shore of the sea to his front door. He was partly aware of, and comforted by, the grip on his right wrist, but the center of his awareness was occupied by a large, cold, gray mass which was pressing down upon him and squeezing out his life with every breath he drew. Rachel was dead. Rachel was dead. Rachel was dead. The words tramped through him keeping time to his footsteps. He kept moving forward, not because he wanted to, but because it was easier, the motion having begun, to continue it than to stop it and do, or not do, something else.

At the house, Jairus was startled by the flute players and the professional mourners already assembled and at work. They would be paid later, in any case, but apparently were hoping to gain a larger fee by being prompt and enthusiastic, for the noise was deafening and the movement was bewildering.

Jairus stopped where he was, just inside the door, unable either to go further into the crowded house or to deal with the eager musicians who, seeing him, redoubled their efforts. Feeling very sorry for Jairus, Simon was about to intervene, by using some of the physical attributes that made him literally the Master's "rock" to silence the din. But that force proved unnecessary.

Stepping forward, still holding the stunned Jairus' wrist Jesus commanded, "Silence!" and a shocked silence stilled the din at once. Into this instant's pool of suspended action Jesus tossed an accurate shepherd's pouch-full of smooth stones: "Why are you making all this racket wailing" he demanded. "The child isn't dead! She's asleep!"

The silence shattered in laughter that was cruelly cold. "Sleeping!" came the hoots of derision. "The brat's as dead as last week's mackerel! Sleeping! It'd take a lot more than us to wake her up! Sleeping!"

A flush rose in Jairus' cheeks as the laughter burned through the fog in which he had been walking, singed his ears and burned a double path, to his mind and to his heart. He was raising his head to speak when Jesus, moving even more effectively through the jeering mob than he himself had done earlier, cleared the professional mourners from the rooms they had managed to fill and closed the great door firmly behind them. He had somehow managed to keep Simon, his rock, James and his brother John, and Jairus, the master of the house, with him inside the dwelling, and to put everyone else out, before anyone had been able to collect sufficient presence of mind to do anything about it. Simon wondered in one unoccupied corner of his mind just how Jesus had managed it all, but he knew that this was not the time to ask.

Rebecca, drawn from her daughter's chamber by the sudden lessening of the mourner's din caused by their enforced departure and the closing of the great door, appeared at the head of the stairs. She had been weeping but now stood dry-eyed and looked at Jesus, who gazed back into her pain-filled eyes, his own darkening in sympathy.

Silently he ascended the staircase, trailed by Jairus, James and John with Simon Peter guarding the rear, checking to make sure none of the disturbers of the peace got back in, and ready to deal with them in his own way if they should do so.

In the doorway of Rachel's room Rebecca stopped. Then she stepped aside and Jesus entered. The others followed him. Standing just inside the doorway, they watched him as he stepped forward. He bent over the bed where Rachel lay. She was even thinner and whiter than Jairus remembered her being when he had

run out of the house that morning, headed for Capernaum and his one last hope--too late, he remembered, and felt again the huge gray stone Benjamin's
message had dropped on his spirits. She was dead.
Why was he bothering the teacher. She was, truly,
dead.

But then, as he heard again the words Jesus had
said, "Only trust, and her life will be spared," he lifted
his head. She must live. Rachel must not be dead! She
must live!

Reaching for Rachel's hand Jesus said in the warm
voice no child had ever, in Simon's experience of him,
been able to resist, "Talitha, get up!" Jairus felt the
hair rise on the back of his neck as he stared at Jesus.
Talitha? Jesus had used the family's name for Rachel,
but he had never been told that that was what they
called her! How had he known to do that?

And then a movement on the bed drew his eyes to
Jesus' hand clasping Rachel's. Color had come back
into her face and her wasted limbs seemed to her
father's astounded eyes to fill out again, and her lusterless hair to shine even as he watched. Her eyelids
fluttered and opened revealing the bright inquiring
gaze he had so loved and had so grieved for during this
strange illness. When Rachel saw Jesus whose words
had roused her from her death-sleep to new life, she
smiled as she began to rise in obedience to his command. Jairus heard a stifled sob beside him. He
turned and saw that the iron control Rebecca had
exercised from the start of Rachel's illness had
crumbled at last. He put his arms around her to
comfort her, and his own tears fell unheeded, wetting
her unbound hair and mourning garb.

"Jairus? Rebecca?" The voice was that of Jesus. As
the couple looked to him, he smiled. Rachel, fully
restored to health was standing with his left arm
around her as she clung to him, gazing at him with all
the love in her heart standing in her eyes. Gently he
detached her from him and turning her toward her
waiting parents gave her a gentle push in their

direction. "She is a beautiful and loving Talitha, your Rachel!" He paused, a smile lighting his eyes and touching his mouth as he watched the girl embrace first her mother and then her father who held her as if he would never let her go. "I think she's probably hungry," he added. "You'd better give her something to eat!"

Rebecca looked at him. "Yes. I will do so at once," she said. "Thank you, sir. You have given us our life." Jairus, looking up to meet his eyes over Rachel's head said, simply," Thank you for giving us our Talitha again."

Moses and the Sea of Reeds

The day was beginning to dawn. For Moses and the 600,000 Israelite men, with their wives, children and cattle encamped at Etham, there were two signs that the night was ending. One was the sudden graying of the east, and the appearance of a faint pink line along the horizon which would almost at once deepen to rose and then to flame and flood the whole eastern sky with light as the sun rose. The second was the fading of the glowing pillar of fire that headed the column of march from the flame--gold that had cheered the night to rose, to pink and then to the pearl gray pillar of cloud that served as their guide by day. It was as if the fire of the pillar became the fire of the sunrise, Moses reflected, and smiled for the first time since his brother Aaron had met him in the wilderness and they had traveled to Egypt together to confront the Pharaoh and obtain the release of the children of Israel as they had been commanded to do by Yahweh. Yahweh seemed to like fire as a sign, thought Moses, and smiled again.

"What's so funny?" The voice was that of Miriam, his and Aaron's older sister. She had joined Moses' family group for the journey, and Aaron, who had his own family to look after, usually managed to spend part of the day with his younger brother and older sister.

"Nothing, really," responded Moses with automatic deference and the faint note of apology that always seemed to creep into his voice when Miriam adopted their mother's commanding tone with him. "I was just watching the sun rise as the pillar changed from fire to cloud again, and thinking how good God has been to us to get us out of Egypt."

"Good! Well, I wonder!" snapped Miriam. She had a headache, due, she supposed, to the accumulation of tension that had been tying all Israel into bowknots while Moses and Aaron struggled with Pharaoh to extract permission from that ruler for all Israel to go into the wilderness to make sacrifice. Now all her fears tumbled out in a biting tirade that made Moses wince and wonder, for the hundredth time since their recent reunion, why on earth Yahweh had saddled him with this impossible woman for a sister and a responsibility.

"Good!" she repeated. "Then, brother dear, tell me why we must run from Egypt like driven rats, carrying packs on our backs and unleavened dough? Why couldn't we have stayed where we were? He could, to hear you tell it, just as easily have killed all the Egyptians and let us take over the cities we built for them, instead of hustling us out in the dark, still swallowing the last mouthful of the strangest meal I ever ate! And what a way to have to eat it--standing up, no less, and dressed for a journey, and then burning perfectly good leftovers that would have made a nice meal the next day! And then, out we pile into those pitch-black streets because Pharaoh finally gets some sense-- we couldn't see our hands in front of our faces! How we were supposed to get ourselves out of that rabbit warren of a city and not lose anyone or leave anyone behind I don't know!"

As she paused for breath, Moses cut in. A mere six weeks experience of Miriam, the sister who had, after all, saved his life (as Zipporah his wife had tactfully reminded him about the third week), had taught Moses that any interruption of Miriam when she was upset and in full spate was worse than useless. Not only would it not change her mind, not silence her, nor even appreciably lower her voice, it seemed to give her fresh energy and several thousand more "other things" to say. But he could not resist. Truth, after all, was truth.

"But we did!" he reminded her. "We did all get out, without losing anyone or leaving behind so much as a lamb! Our God is good to us! He created the pillar of fire to lead us by night, and it changes to a pillar of cloud to shelter and lead us by day!"

"You are a fool!" snorted his sister. Her headache was piercing through the center of her left eye-socket all the way out to the base of her skull and then return- ing to its point of origin in two iron bands, one running around the left side of her head just behind the ear to her nose, and the other travelling up over her head on the mid-line of her skull and joining the first at the nose with a hollow clang that reverberated all the way to the pit of her stomach.

"Why am I a fool?" asked Moses, as Miriam appear- ed ready to let the matter drop with the thud of her judgement. He bit his tongue in vexation. His very ask- ing of the question had just proved Miriam's point, he thought wryly. He had had her silence, if rancorous, within his grasp, and had forfeited this tenuous peace for the sake of an idle thrust. Now he was for it!

He was not wrong. "*Why* you are a fool I do not know!" his sister declared with some energy. "Perhaps your precious Princess dropped you on your head after Mother and I brought you to the palace! Perhaps the Egyptian magicians turned your brain into a frog's! I don't know! But I can tell you *how* you are foolish! You say God is good to us by bringing us all out of Egypt and by keeping us together by using this fire-and-cloud pillar. Wonderful! Brother, dear," cooed the irate sis- ter, her tone a perfect blend of acid in honey, "has it ever occurred to you that if we can see each other and find our route in the light and sight of this precious pillar you and God have concocted, so can the Egyptians? I tell you, you are a fool! We might as well have stayed where we were! Pharaoh's no giant intellect, but all he has to do is look, and he can find us and come to get us any time he wants!"

"But," Moses interrupted again, though everything within him warned him to be still, and his bitten tongue tried to cooperate by stuttering, "b-b-b-but, Pharaoh l-l-let us go! He even c-c-c-commanded us to go. Right then and there! And God knew he would," he added, the memory of the event of two nights ago sweeping him past both his residual fear of Miriam and the rising terrors her harsh words had evoked in him. "That's why He commanded us to eat standing, staff in hand, dressed for a journey, and why he had us pack up all the silver and gold the Egyptians gave us, and why He had us burn the leftovers."

"Yes, Pharaoh let us go," Miriam agreed, but the acid-in-honey tone sharpened ominously. Moses waited. He was afraid to listen to what she was certainly going to say, yet, like the bird, sitting fascinated before the snake about to kill it, he could not speak to silence her, nor could he move away from her. Inexorably she went on. "*Let* us go. For the moment, brother dear. How many times did he refuse to let us go? Nine, wasn't it? And how many times did your plagues force him to 'let us go' before? Only five. And each of those times, what happened? The minute that the plague you and Aaron and that staff of yours had brought was gone--'No!' he'd say, 'They can't go!' What makes you think, my Egyptian pet, that it's going to be any different this time? He'll never let us go, staff or no staff, deaths or no deaths, and that pillar might just as well be an open invitation to him. When he wakes up and realizes we've gone, Pharaoh will be after us like an arrow. And mark my words, that 'protective pillar' of Yahweh will light him straight to his target! You are a fool of fools, dear brother! Now leave me alone. I have a headache that, if I'm lucky, will kill me before Pharaoh gets here. And don't deceive yourself," she tossed over her shoulder as she stooped to enter her tent, "he's coming, and neither you, nor Aaron, nor that stupid staff, nor God can stop him. You wait and see!"

It was a good thing no one, not even the redoubtable Miriam in a towering rage, could slam a tent flap, Moses reflected, for the report would have told the Pharaoh exactly where they were even if he had been asleep with a pillow over his head! The smile that had touched his mouth and eyes with the dawn returned. Poor thing, he thought, how much pain she made for herself. And for others, he added, and felt again the burden Miriam's diatribe had dropped on his spirits. "Rest if you can," he murmured after her, knowing they would have to be moving on soon.

"What was that all about?" inquired a quiet voice behind him. The gentle, somewhat amused tones belonged to Aaron, Moses' brother, his senior by three years, and his staunchest friend, though the two men had only met again some six weeks earlier, when Yahweh had brought them together to free Israel from Pharaoh. "Sister Dear on the rampage again?" the voice went on sweetly, the laughter just under the surface. This name for Miriam had been Aaron's invention years before, an ironic echo-response to Miriam's invariable form of address to him, "Brother Dear" when she was angry. When Moses had rejoined the family, Miriam had simply extended the name to him as well, and from that point on, Miriam was "Sister Dear" to both her brothers, though only when they were in private and she was safely out of earshot! Miriam did not bully Aaron, having learned by bitter experience over the years, that while she could not goad him into losing his temper, his wit or his train of thought no matter what she said, nor how she said it, he could, and did, merrily turn any argument she cared to raise upside down and inside out, unraveling it as he went, and transforming it into some comic absurdity that he could blithely hang around her neck. Then he would walk away laughing, and she, when she had sputtered her way to raging incoherence, would have to go to bed for a day with one of her headaches.

"Yes," responded Moses, gloomily.

"What is it this time," asked Aaron lightly. "Tent drafty? Road too dusty? Pillar of fire shines in her eyes so she can't sleep at night? Staff makes her nervous? Too bad I can't turn it loose on her! Show her what a real snake can do! Maybe it'd convince her not to try and be one with you!"

"Aaron!" reproved Moses automatically. "You mustn't say things like that. She does get those awful headaches, and she says things she doesn't really mean."

"I hope not!" rejoined Aaron. "Calling you a fool and Yahweh as good as one, or maybe even a traitor--that's enough to put her in real danger from Yahweh that'll make his treatment of Pharaoh look like a love-tap you'd give a child! Miriam really must learn to govern her tongue. You want me to tackle her?" Real concern had suffused Aaron's voice as the rose-gold suffused the dawn sky, and Moses turned to his brother with love and gratitude.

"No," he said. "Let her be. She's in too much pain to be able to listen or understand what she's done, and she'll only make matters worse. Besides," he went on, and the worry that had been edging his voice now emerged fully, "I need to talk to you."

"Sure," agreed the older brother. "What about?"

"Our situation," replied Moses. I know Miriam's-- well, not altogether reliable these days."

"That's an understatement!" his brother interjected with a grin. Then, "Go on," he said. "I'm sorry I inter- rupted you."

"Well, but she said that, with the pillar of cloud-and- fire, we would make a perfect target for Pharaoh if he changes his mind again and decides to come after us and re-enslave us. And we would. We do!"

"Don't you think Yahweh can figure that out too, if Sister Dear can see it? Don't worry! He went to all the trouble of springing us from Egypt, with a full load of silver and gold don't forget! He's not going to let anybody mess things up for him now--not Pharaoh, not Miriam, not us, and certainly not His pillar of fire-and- cloud! Relax! Grab some sleep! You need it, if Sister Dear can scramble your thinking and confidence that badly!" Aaron grasped his younger brother's shoulder and shook it lightly. "Relax!" he said again, smiling. "Yahweh's in charge! You want me to prove it with the staff?"

"Thanks, no!" said Moses quickly, smiling in return, but glancing around him for the staff in spite of himself. "Where--"

"In my tent--still a staff!" Aaron assured him.

"Now, will you let Yahweh be God, and stop trying to take on the job yourself? He made Pharaoh--let Him deal with him! And the same goes for Miriam--double! In fact, only Yahweh *can* handle Sister Dear--so let's let Him do it!"

Moses laughed at that, and, invisibly, Aaron relaxed. It was the laughter he had been working toward, for he knew that once Moses was far enough back from the edge of whatever troubles boiled around them to laugh, even at something as small as the notion of Yahweh dealing with Miriam, he would once again be open to hear the voice of Yahweh and to speak it to Israel. That connection, Aaron knew without being told, had to be maintained, or the whole people would perish.

"I guess the rest will have to wait," Moses was responding. He pointed to the pillar of cloud, now translucent pearl throughout. "He's telling us to pack up and move on," he explained and Aaron nodded.

"I'll rouse Miriam," he offered, "and get her settled in a litter. You get the rest started."

Moses nodded. "Thanks," he said, "for everything." He met Aaron's eyes for a long moment, then turned to mobilize the exiles. In half-an-hour, more or less, the whole camp was on the move, following the luminescent cloud.

At the noonday break, when all the people were at rest, Yahweh spoke to Moses. "Tell the sons of Israel to turn back and pitch camp in front of Pi-hahiroth, between Migdol and the sea, facing Baal-zephon. You are to pitch your camp opposite this place, beside the sea."

Moses blinked. Turn back? Why, then, had the Lord led them here, using the cloud to guide them? And what was so special about Pi-hahiroth and a camp facing the sea? What was the point of this maneuver?

By this time, of course, Moses knew enough not to voice his questions and doubts; Yahweh always had reasons, even if He sometimes chose not to reveal them. This time, however, it appeared He did choose, for, as if

Moses had spoken aloud, Yahweh responded, explaining, "Pharaoh will think, 'Look how these sons of Israel wander to and fro in the countryside; the wilderness has closed in on them.' Then I shall make Pharaoh's heart stubborn, and he will set out in pursuit of them."

Moses, listening intently, jumped at the last words. So Miriam, Sister Dear, had been partly right! Pharaoh would pursue them! But if Yahweh already knew this, why--? He did not have a chance to finish the unspoken question. Yahweh was continuing, "But I shall win glory for myself at the expense of Pharaoh and all his army, and the Egyptians will learn that I amYahweh."

As the heat of the day eased and the camp began to stir Moses gave them the orders the Lord had given him, but did not mention the coming pursuit by the Pharaoh's forces nor Yahweh's intention to gain glory at Egypt's expense. For one thing, he had no idea how the Lord intended to gain His glory, nor what would be expected of him and his fellow-Israelites in the process. And for a second, his confrontation with Miriam had convinced him that it would be wiser to let the Egyptians do their own advance publicity, or, better still, to arrive unheralded.

For where Miriam had been furious, both with him and with God, she had not been in the least frightened, but he was not sure his 600,000 ex-slaves, with their wives and children, if they knew in advance of the coming of pursuing Egyptian forces, would not bolt in panic into the desert the second they saw the first chariot, or, more likely, simply surrender themselves to the arriving Egyptians and march back into slavery without the hint of a struggle. The second possibility, in fact, had been the reason Yahweh had given him for forbidding the Israelites to take the northern road to the land of the Philistines, though it was the shorter route into Canaan, the land Yahweh had promised to Abraham and his descendants.

Moses set his jaw grimly. He was determined that,

no matter what price he and they had to pay, Israel would not fail Yahweh that way. After all the trouble He had taken to free them from Egyptian slavery, they would not turn back to it.

As they moved toward the place Yahweh had selected for their camp as the site of His glorification, Moses was remembering the past forty-five days of war and miracles by which Yahweh had persuaded Pharaoh that he would be better off without his slave-labor force. Moses shook his head and smiled silently. Yahweh was indeed the God of gods, the one Lord of the universe.

Aaron, walking beside his brother, seemed to be reading his mind, for at this point he broke into Moses' train of thought. "You never can tell," he remarked, "exactly what the Lord has in mind when He gives you an order, can you? You know it's best, but you can't always see why, or how He's going to work everything out."

Moses looked sharply at his brother, probing his eyes for an instant to see if there were any particular trouble prompting the remarks, but finding nothing except alert intelligence and kindness in Aaron's eyes, contented himself with a non-commital grunt which could have been either yes or no.

The reply seemed to satisy Aaron, who was in any case preoccupied with his own musings. He went on, "Remember the first time we went to Pharaoh? Even when we did and said all Yahweh commanded, Pharaoh didn't budge. Instead he cut off the supplies of straw to our brickmakers, but ordered them to produce the same number of bricks daily, though they had to find their own straw. Then, when they couldn't, Pharaoh had the overseers beat the Hebrew foremen, and wouldn't listen to their complaints. We almost got killed that time; the people blamed us for Pharaoh's insane rage and sadistic slave-drivers, and if it hadn't been for the wonders He told us to work, we wouldn't be alive today, I'm convinced! Now why didn't He start out with the wonders? That's what I want to know.

Any one of them would have gotten us a better hearing from Pharaoh, and a better reputation with our own, somewhat dense people..."

"Sheep" interjected Moses.

"You're right!" agreed Aaron. "And you can't get milk, wool or meat from them either."

"Maybe it's because the Israelites--well, let's be honest and say we--are so thick-headed, so sheep-dense, that Yahweh has to do these elaborate demonstrations," offered Moses. "Maybe the wonders are mostly done to teach *us* that He is God, the only God there is or can be; maybe Pharaoh and his people are only part of the demonstration to show us what He means by fidelity and love and keeping promises, so we can learn how to be His people, as He is our God?"

"How do you mean?" The usually quick-witted Aaron was caught off balance by this unusual view. "You mean, Yahweh turned all the water in Egypt into blood, even the water in the jars, so that *we* would learn--learn what?"

"That He is God, the only One, I presume," returned Moses, "and that we are His people."

"How?" demanded Aaron. "It didn't work. Pharaoh didn't even say he'd let us go that time. He just stomped back into the palace, slammed the door in our faces and ignored the whole thing. He thought we were second-best to his magicians because they could turn water to blood, too. And he ignored us and the blood for seven whole days! What did that teach us?"

"Not to challenge Yahweh or refuse Him what He asks for, for one thing. At least I hope it taught us that," he added grimly. "But I'm not sure it did. It also showed us a kind of power none of us had ever imagined--at least I hadn't."

"Not even after the burning bush?" asked Aaron.

"Not even after the burning bush," his brother agreed." That was a special gift to me, but it came as love not force, and so I didn't look for force when we came to Egypt. Pharaoh may not have been scared of our God--but I think he was terrified and trying to hide it. If he wasn't scared of Yahweh, why didn't he have us killed the second he felt threatened or insulted by our message? No, take it from me, Pharaoh was scared of the Lord God, and was meant to be, so he'd learn some respect--and so were we. Meant to be, that is. As I say, I'm not at all that sure it's worked on us."

"Apparently it hasn't on Miriam," offered Aaron, and Moses smiled wryly.

"Sister Dear doesn't scare easily, nor does she respect anyone besides herself until he proves his right to respect by knocking her flat," he opined. "That's why she respects you and stays out of your way, while she's still trying to trample me into the dust."

"I have never laid a finger on our Miriam!" protested Aaron. "Not even once! Not even when she was being REALLY impossible! Not that I didn't want to, especially when you'd gone off to be the Princess' pet Hebrew, and I was the only little brother she had. But Mama would've reduced me to a thin layer of paste and spread me all over Goshen if I'd even thought such a thing when she was around, so I repressed my baser instincts and treated Miriam like a lady even though she was anything but! So what do you mean I knocked her flat?"

Moses was laughing by this time, both at the picture of their mother spreading Aaron with a knife-blade over the land of Goshen, and of Aaron treating a frothing Miriam like a lady. When he got his breath he said, "Calm down! I meant that figuratively. But you have, at some point in your mutual history, convinced Sister Dear that tangling with a brace of lions is preferable to crossing verbal swords with you. How did you do it? I'd like to know, for my own information!"

"Well," said Aaron doubtfully and then stopped. A smile curved into a sudden laugh and a head-shake. "You're right! I did flatten her once--" he admitted, "but that was years ago, and, well, it's a long story! I can't tell you now, but if you ever really need to know, I'll find a way."

"I know you will," his brother assured him with a

nod. "Still," he added with a grin, "I'd like to have been there!"

Aaron's eyebrows flicked up once and levelled, but he resisted the temptation so artfully presented by his brother and held his tongue. Gradually the reminiscent delight faded as present concerns reasserted their claims. "Moses?" he began after a long but companionable silence.

"What is it?" his brother inquired with a measure of concern. It was not often that the controlled, polished Aaron allowed himself the luxury of revealing uncertainty, and still less fear. Both were being shown him now, Moses knew, and he rallied all his forces to meet them and give Aaron back the strength his brother had given him so fully and freely during the recent ordeal.

"Moses, it's not over yet, is it?"

Moses heard the question with his ears, but it registered more like a sharp blow to the diaphragm. He caught his breath with the force of the fear which the question, spoken aloud, had released.

"No," he said simply. "It's not."

"Thank you!" said Aaron, and the relief in his voice was so plain and so full of gratitude that the younger man wheeled on him sharply.

"I said no, it's not over," he repeated. "You did understand that?"

"Yes!" said Aaron. "That's what I asked you!"

"Then what are you so happy about?" demanded Moses, his voice crackling with baffled annoyance. "I say we're still in the soup and you sing, 'Pass me a cracker. This is fun!' I don't get it! I just don't understand you!"

"You don't," agreed Aaron, "but that's not your fault. You haven't lived with Mama and Miriam all your life! If you had, you'd realize what a miracle of light and peace a simple, direct answer to a hard question can be! I asked you the hardest question a man can ask of his leader, or of his brother. I asked you to tell me the truth about our situation--the situation you,

ultimately, must deal with and answer for--when that
truth was a negative one. And you did! You told me
without excuses, or hysterics, or recriminations, or
evasions, or accusations, or any of the thousand other
inventions and evasions humans have developed to
avoid saying the truths they need and cannot bear to
hear and say."

"Slow down!" said Moses. "Of course I told you the
truth! And you got a simple no because, in spite of a
life's training in Egyptian deviousness and court
etiquette, when a man is brave enough to show me his
fear of what may be the case, and to ask to have that
fear confirmed if it must be, I cannot deny him the
whole truth, nor will I extend the misery of his
uncertainty by so much as a syllable if I can avoid
doing so." Putting his hands on Aaron's shoulders,
the younger man gripped them lightly and gave his
brother a slight, affectionate shake. "Remember me?"
he said. "I'm your younger brother, not your older
sister!"

"Pleased to meet you--again!" Aaron responded
more cheerfully. "But about that whole truth..."

"What about it?" asked Moses quietly. "What do you
want to know?"

"Anything you know--and want to tell me," replied
Aaron.

"Why don't you tell me what you know, or have
figured out? That'll be easier in the long run, I think."
He turned to continue walking, putting his right arm
over his brother's shoulder as he did so, so that the two
traveled in comradely union as they talked.

"Well," began Aaron, "When I asked you if it was
over, I meant the slavery to Pharaoh. What I was
thinking was, here we are, 600,000 men strong--well,"
he amended seeing Moses raised eyebrows and somewhat sardonic smile, "600,000 men in number, then,
marching with our wives, our children and our beasts
out into the wilderness all by ourselves. We're not on
the usual route to Canaan, so we're still well within
range of Pharaoh, if he decides he wants us back. And

if he does, what then? It's all very well to work wonders when we all know where we are, but this way,
well, where do we go if he backs off again? And what
do we do if he doesn't?"

"Now you've been listening to Sister Dear," Moses
interrupted, smiling, and gave his brother's shoulder a
gentle squeeze with his right hand then released him
with a pat on the back. "What's that in front of your
nose that shows you where to put each foot down?" he
demanded.

"The Pillar of Cloud by day and of Fire by night that
is the Lord," replied Aaron at once. "Yes, I know He's
here, and He's in charge. I just finished telling you so.
But what about Pharaoh? He will come after us you
know--he always has. What about Pharaoh?"

"What about him?" repeated his brother. "Aaron,
what's the matter with you? How many wonders did
you work, at Yahweh's command, with that staff and
only His words? I mean it! Recite them for me so I'm
sure you remember them and don't start thinking you
only dreamed them and that maybe they never happened! No, do it," he insisted as Aaron began to shake
his head in demurral. "I think it's important."

"Well, let's see, then," began his brother, counting
on his fingers. He was, as Moses had hoped he might
be, momentarily distracted from his preoccupation
with the imponderables of Pharaoh's reactions and
possible retaliatory measures.

"There was the waters being turned into blood. That
was first. On that one, Pharaoh's magicians duplicat-
ed the effect by a trick, and Pharaoh just slammed into
the palace, refusing even to listen to us.

"And seven days later--there were all those frogs.
Was that the second one?"

"Yes," Moses affirmed. "The Lord sent us to
Pharaoh to warn him first, and then told you to stretch
out your hand and the staff over the streams and
canals."

"Which I did," interrupted Aaron. "I've never seen
so many frogs in all my life! It was just like what the

message we gave Pharaoh said! There were frogs everywhere, teeming in the river, coming up into the palace, in the bedroom, on Pharaoh's very bed, in the servant's houses, in the homes of his subjects--even in the ovens and kneading bowls! It was incredible! Now that time we got some action! But it didn't last. I wonder if the magicians' success had anything to do with it?"

"I don't really think so," said his brother thoughtfully. "Pharaoh did send for us to ask us to ask our God to remove the frogs. If he'd thought it was just magic, he wouldn't have bothered. And he certainly wouldn't have promised to let us go as his part of the bargain."

"But once God did take the frogs away," Aaron objected, "Pharaoh changed his mind again! If he'd believed it was God, he wouldn't have done that. You'd think with fourteen tons of dead frogs heaped up everywhere he looked, stinking piles just rotting in the broiling sun, Pharaoh would have believed that God had sent them, and that God had taken them away again. And you'd think he would have figured out why! After all, you just can't call that many frogs, dead or alive, an illusion or a magician's trick, no matter how much you and your magicians may want to!"

"You can get around that, though," Moses reminded him. "You can simply not name the frogs at all! That way, you don't have to say cause or effect--or acknowledge any, who, at all!"

"Maybe you *do* know Miriam!" his brother murmured. "That's how she operates all the time!"

"So does Pharaoh, I think!" said Moses. "But go on with the list." Obediently Aaron continued, "Well, then it was the gnats, wasn't it?"

"Yes," Moses agreed. "You were to strike the dust of the earth with your staff so it would be turned into gnats throughout all Egypt."

"That was when we, God, I mean, knocked the magicians flat!" Aaron recalled gleefully. "They couldn't raise a single gnat, and we raised zillions of them! Gnats just infested every human being and every beast in Egypt! I was sure Pharaoh would get rid of us then!"

"That time he didn't even listen to our message," Moses reminded him, "in spite of the fact that his own magicians told him the gnats came by the finger of God."

"He is a stubborn one--no mistake," Aaron agreed.

"Just like us!" said Moses.

"Us?" asked Aaron.

"Israelites," Moses explained. "Did you notice any great outpouring of loyalty and trust when the 'bricks without straw' order went through? And they had seen the wonders God worked through us! Sheep, I tell you! Stick their noses in a stream and their feet in green grass, and they'll drink and eat; tell them they've got to go over to the other side of the hill or wait until to-morrow and they'll panic--or kill you!" he ended bitterly.

Aaron looked at his brother narrowly. Neither the intensity in Moses' tone nor his judgement of the Israelites could be satisfactorily accounted for by what they had seen of their extended kindred to date.

The Israelites had observed the ritual meal with its strange prescriptions which Yahweh had commanded very carefully, without objection. They had quickly moved out of Egypt when the order went out, even though the night was dark, and the eerie wailing of the Egyptians filled the countryside. There was not an Egyptian family, highborn or low, free or slave, human or animal, that had not lost its firstborn, and the grieving had an element of the terrifying in its un-iversality, as well as in its abandon. Yet no one of the Hebrews, no man or woman or child, had so much as whimpered. He observed quietly, "That sounds more like what you're afraid will happen than what has actually happened so far. What's up?" And then, as his brother hesitated, he insisted, "I have to know, Moses, if I'm going to find ways to help you in this mission. Otherwise, our God isn't going to get His people freed and in their own land in one piece. And that is simply not acceptable. Besides, it'd be an awful waste of His time--an insult, really. And you said the whole truth!"

"Agreed," said Moses at last. "I was going to tell you all of it anyway when you'd finished reciting the wonders--and that's not just a way to shut you up," he added. "It's important for both of us to keep in mind just Who our God is. You're worried about Pharaoh and the Egyptians, and I'm worried about our people and their slave-mentality. Between us, we can totally blot out the reality of Yahweh even though we're walking in the light of his pillar of fire or in the shadow of his cloud!"

Aaron nodded his comprehension. "Well, then," he suggested, "suppose I get on with the list?"

"Please," said his brother gratefully. "I think I need to hear it all said out loud right about now."

"The flies came next," Aaron began. "I tend to think of that as the second phase of God's campaign, or demonstration, if you prefer."

"Demonstration," said Moses. "But how do you mean 'second phase'? What was different about the flies? You warned Pharaoh what would happen to him if he didn't let us, His people, go to worship Him. Though why He should bother with us I don't know!" he finished.

"Let's save that question for after the list, as we're doing with my anxieties," suggested Aaron gently. It was not like Moses to fret, and his older brother knew the man within the leader God had created must be troubled indeed to allow himself to be so distracted.

As Moses nodded and mumbled an abrupt "Sorry!" Aaron continued. "The differences weren't all that obvious to anybody outside, I suppose," he agreed, "but I certainly noticed! For one thing, I didn't use the staff to summon them!"

"So you didn't!" Moses agreed with some surprise. "I'd forgotten! Or maybe I just wasn't noticing that much. You told Pharaoh the flies would come if he didn't release us--"

"And that the sign would take place on the next day," Aaron concluded. "That was it! No staff, no raw material--just the Lord's word and the promise, and then, the next day, flies by the million! But there was another difference about the sign. Do you remember?"

"N-no-" said Moses hesitantly. "I don't think so."

"Just think!" urged his brother. "Repeat what the Lord told us to say to Pharaoh after the part about the flies--or shall I?"

"You do it," said Moses. "The words are your department in this mission. Besides, I think I need to listen to this."

"Well, right after the graphic description of the flies covering the very ground on which the Egyptians were standing, He said we were to say, 'But on that day I will make an exception of the land of Goshen: There shall be no flies where My people dwell, that you may know that I am the Lord in the midst of the earth. I will make this distinction between My people and your people!'"

"That you may know that I am the Lord in the midst of the earth!" Moses repeated slowly. "Yes. That's what it's all been about all along. And still is, I guess. Thank you Aaron. That was good to hear."

"And to say," agreed his brother energetically. "I mean it," he said in response to Moses' wordless look of inquiry. "God is in charge. And, you're right, we are worse than sheep! But anyway, there was another difference with the flies that we haven't looked at."

"That being?"

"Pharaoh's reaction! He cracked! Well, he sort of split in a couple of places, if you won't have 'cracked'! Remember? That was the first time he acknowledged that we had a real God Who had a right to our services, Who had real claims on us."

"Yes, but look how he did it!" exclaimed Moses. "First it was, 'Offer a sacrifice in this country!' And then, when I wouldn't have that--"

"You did a nice job getting us out of it, by the way," Aaron interrupted. "I meant to tell you, but things were moving kind of fast at that point."

"Not my doing!" Moses responded. "That was Yahweh, pure and simple! Anyhow, when I refused that ploy by saying we'd anger the Egyptians who would consider our sacrifices an abomination, and that the Lord had commanded us to go a three-days, journey into the desert to offer Him the sacrifice, he said all right, but that we couldn't go too far! That's cracking? That's splitting? That's not even getting a pinhole! That man is a horror! He never cracked! He never will."

"You're beginning to sound like me, now!" remarked Aaron, trying to break Moses' anger and fear with a touch of laughter. "Don't forget, the flies made him ask us to pray for him to our God when we went to offer sacrifice! And," he continued riding over Moses' objection, "though he reversed himself again and refused to let us go, once you had prayed to God and He had removed every single fly, he wasn't as hard to get to the next time."

"A distinction without a difference!" growled Moses. "But you're right. And I suppose where Yahweh is concerned, every step you take forward is one less you still have to take. All right. I see the difference in the flies. But a second stage?"

"Israelites spared what Egyptians are suffering, even though they're both in the same place at the same time--as a sign of Yahweh's power!"

"How?" demanded Moses. "We were in the Goshen countryside. The Egyptians and the flies were in the cities where the Egyptians lived!"

"What fly did you ever meet that recognized city limits?" demanded Aaron, torn between amusement and impatience. "Flies are like tribesmen in Canaan-- wherever they settle and don't get swatted out of is their place! Don't tell me you really think the flies wouldn't have blanketed us just as thickly as they did the Egyptians, except that Yahweh prevented it!"

"Well, no," admitted Moses, with the start of a rueful grin.

"Then you acknowledge that our fly-free condition was a real sign of Yahweh's protective power?"

"Yes," said Moses. "I do."

"Well, that sign, or that kind of sign is the mark of the whole of what I'm calling the second stage of Yahweh's camp--demonstration. In the plague, re-member"?

"Their cattle and livestock got it. Ours .didn't," Moses affirmed. "Yes. I see what you mean. And then the boils..."

"Again. They got them, and we didn't," said Aaron. "And even their magicians got those boils. So much for their powers!"

"So that's why they stopped showing up!" exclaimed Moses.

"Of course!" his brother replied. "If a magician can't even keep other people's magic from giving him boils, how much credit do you think he'll have with anybody else? Especially Pharaoh, who, as we have both noticed from time to time, is an extremely practical individual, besides having a head as hard as a pyramid stone where penetration by a new idea is concerned. And let me tell you, the idea of any god he can't control is extremely new to the Pharaoh--so new, and so re-pellent, that he blocks it out, even as he's wading knee-deep in the effects of that God's power!"

"That's why he worries you, isn't it?" asked Moses. "Not because you doubt Yahweh, but because you think Pharaoh will never quit--not even after that last blow."

"Yes," admitted Aaron uncomfortably, "I haven't forgotten what he told us to tell old Hard-head before that punishing hail storm, either. Did you notice, by the way, how He took care to warn them to get the poor beasts under shelter before the storm? That's a touch I hadn't expected."

"That's like Him," said Moses. "He never has been a God for indiscriminate destruction. Remember Abra-ham and the bargaining about just men? And though there were only Lot and his family, five instead of the ten just men agreed on, God still rescued poor old Lot."

"Practically in spite of himself!" agreed Aaron. "Did you ever hear of such a silly and stubborn man? Wouldn't go as far as the mountains even though all Gehenna was poised to rain down on Sodom and Gomorrah practically under his sandal-soles! And that wife of his! Stubborn? Amazing!"

"Sister Dear!" murmured Moses, in spite of himself. At Aaron's hoot of laughter he added, more seriously, "There's more than one Lot, silly, fearful and stubborn, among our 600,000 men you know. Sometimes," he went on in a tone so low Aaron could scarcely hear him, "I find more of old Lot in myself than I can bear."

"No," said Aaron firmly, and reached for his brother's hand. Gripping it he declared, "You get tired sometimes, and worried. But you're no fool. And though you may be afraid, you trust Yahweh absolutely. So you're stubborn in only one way--you'll do what He says, as He says it, or die trying."

With a final grip and slight shake he let go of Moses' hand, but not before he heard the murmured "Thanks," Moses was able to get out.

"Now let's get back to that hail storm!" Aaron commanded, and Moses nodded. "It's the start of the third stage of the demonstration," the older man went on. "This was where Yahweh even had us explain to Pharaoh *why* He was sending punishment on the Egyptians as the painful consequences of Pharaoh's disobedience, in stages, rather than demolishing them all at once."

"Oh, yes!" Moses broke in. "I remember exactly the words you were told to say. 'But this is why I have spared you; to show you My power and to make My Name resound throughout the earth!'"

"And even after that, and that incredible hailstorm that flattened everything it hit, Pharaoh didn't really believe God is God. Yes, he grovelled and begged and said he was a sinner and said we could go. All he really wanted was for the thunder and hail to stop."

"I knew that," said Moses, somewhat testily. "Why do you think I told him I would pray as soon as I had left the city? I even told him I knew he and his servants didn't yet fear God."

"Yes," returned his brother, "and it didn't daunt him a bit. It didn't embarrass him to be so two-faced, and it didn't even make him a little nervous to try to deal with God that way."

"No, of course not. You see," Moses explained, "Egyptians, or at least Pharaoh's kind, regard everything as for sale, outside of their own religious rites, and even those--well, I don't know. The Egyptians are a devious bunch. For precise mathematicians and astronomers, they have the most astonishing notions about accuracy in other areas! Truth is one among many equally acceptable, equally useful weapons in the arsenal. In this court, for this Pharaoh, 'the good' is anything that accomplishes his will and achieves his ends, and anything that would thwart or inhibit his will is 'evil.' Whether what is said is true or not is irrelevant, and promises are simply expedients, levers to move whatever obstacles may block his way to his ends. So giving his word is a matter of expending so much air for Pharaoh--no more and no less. And to accuse him of lying of acting in bad faith is to speak a foreign language to him. Honesty and honorable conduct, as we understand such things, are meaningless to Pharaoh. That was one of the things I learned from my years as the Princess' pet Hebrew. I understood it early, but I never was comfortable playing that game."

"Well, if you know all that," demanded Aaron, "and have known it all along, why aren't you nervous about Pharaoh coming after us now? He reneged on his repentance and promise once the hail stopped; why won't he do the same thing now?"

"Well, the children are dead, for one thing, and while nobody else is dying, the dead ones are going to stay dead. There's no reversal possible in this last one, none at all. And there's always the possibility of more deaths if he does renege. But you said something about the hail starting the third stage of Yahweh's demonstration. How?"

"Well, it was with the hail that the Lord started saying that all this was being done not just for us, or for Pharaoh, but so that His Name might be revered over the whole earth. No god has ever pushed a claim that far. And it was while the hail was killing everyone and everything exposed to it that Pharaoh decided to let us go, on condition we pray for him and get the hail stopped. That only lasted until the skies cleared, of course, but it was further than he'd ever gone before. Then, when the locusts came and actually began to devour every speck of green in the country, because Pharaoh would not agree to let us all go, but only the men, the people turned against Pharaoh and told him he was gettig the nation destroyed by his stubbornness-- though they were somewhat more tactful than that."

"The locusts and this Egyptian reaction were for our benefit," Moses reminded him, "so our people would see his glory and know that He alone is Lord. And I'm not sure it worked for us, though it really shook the Pharaoh's complacency. Sorry--I didn't mean to inter- rupt. Go on about the third stage."

"I think," Aaron went on, "that when He sent the hail and the locusts, God escalated His offensive campaign, so that He attacked not only the property of men and their bodies but the very sources of the people's life. All the standing crops were flattened by the hail--and, you recall, the flax was in bud and the barley had eared when the storm came. Then the locusts ate up the rising wheat and spelt, as well as every leaf that greened in the whole country. That meant the trees and bushes would die and all Egypt would be a bare sand desert."

"So the Egyptians lost both present as well as future food supplies in those two punishments," interjected Moses, "and that's why they turned on Pharaoh, adding political unrest and the threat of anarchy to the economic and agricultural disasters that had begun to swallow up Egypt."

"Yes,"   Aaron   agreed.   "Those two punishments

alone, unchecked, would have been the end of the nation with the countryside that had supported it. So Pharaoh had to give in, as the people demanded, at least for the moment. He had no choice, and even he could see that much. But I think he figured if he could get the pun-ishment stopped in time, so that he could salvage even some of the grain and green, he might be able to keep the country alive, to hold it together and to retain his throne. And then he could do as he liked with us."

"What about the next-to-last punishment, though-- after the locusts were gone and Pharaoh reneged again? I still don't see what was so terrible about dark- ness, even three days of it, that He saved it all that time," said Moses thoughtfully. "I know it pushed Pharaoh another step toward com-pliance, so he was willing to release all the people--though not the livestock-but I don't see why it worked."

"That's because the sun continued to shine for us! Use your imagination!" Aaron challenged him.

"I can't. I haven't got any, or at least not much," said Moses simply. "I never have had. I guess that's why I killed the Egyptian overseer when I was first coming to terms with the fact that the Hebrews were my people."

"And that's why you never expected the Hebrews' response to your murder of their oppressor, I guess," Aaron put in.

"Mmm," Moses agreed.

"Well, use my imagination then," Aaron proposed. "That's a quality of which I have a good supply---an oversupply as Sister Dear is fond of reminding me. She thinks imagination makes men cowards. I say it keeps them alive and ensures that the life they live is a truly human one, not just a beast's waking, feeding, coupl- ing and sleeping, with a fight or two to keep turf lines straight."

"I suspect you may both have a piece of a much larger truth," suggested Moses, "but at the moment, I can't think. Tell me, why did the darkness work? It didn't bend a gnat's wing!"

"Darkness isolates," began Aaron slowly. "It separates a man from every other human being in the world and seals him up inside himself. And then it begins to separate him from himself. He no longer knows what's real and what's not. First he's separated from his own body. The knowledge that comes to him about himself in relation to the world around him through his senses is blocked out, so he quite literally does not know whether he's on his head or his feet. He doesn't know up from down, front from back, left from right--and pretty soon he doesn't know inside from outside--his own sensations from the things around him that cause these sensations. All distinctions disappear in a swirl--hot and cold, wet and dry, hard and soft--all lose meaning, and all equally bewilder him. Leave a man long enough in this darkness that can practically be felt, and he will go mad and be destroyed by his own unhinged perceptions. Believe me," Aaron ended his description, "I'd rather have locusts, flies and gnats all at once, with a helping of hail and blood for water, any day of the week than that darkness even for a day! And Pharaoh got his Egyptians three full days of it!"

Moses shivered. "If one of the benefits of an imagination is being able to summon up a horror like that, without having experienced it," he said quietly, "I'm rather glad I haven't got one. How did any of them survive it?"

"They haven't got all that much imagination either, I guess," Aaron offered after a moment's thought. "In fact," he added, "I think that's why Pharaoh can keep having his nose shoved into the effects of Yahweh's power being used against him and still not catch on to the fact that he can't win against the Lord if the Lord refuses to allow him to."

"You mean," asked Moses, "his Egyptian deviousness isn't really cleverness but blindness? That for him nothing is real except what's happening now, so in a crisis he says and does whatever will take the pressure off, and as soon as things are back to normal he forgets there ever *was* a crisis, and why?"

"Yes," Aaron affirmed. "That's what I said! He has no imagination. The past is always, and only, past for him--and it's over; it has no applications in the present. And the future will be what he chooses it to be. He just can't envision a successful challenge to his claims to godhead, on the theoretical level, or to his grip on absolute, all-but universal power on the practical level. And that 's why I'm so worried now. I really don't believe even that final punishment will have a lasting effect. It can't! Pharaoh simply hasn't the capacity to project the terrors that will come upon him if he persists in this madness of defying Yahweh, even with ten, shall we say, graphic examples within his own experience. He's noticed the escalation of consequences. That's why each time he conceded a little more of what Yahweh was asking. But he can see neither its significance nor the consequences for him and Egypt if he continues to war against God. When he turns to the future, all he sees is a blank white wall, and he's such an egotist he takes a brush and writes his name on it instead of trying to picture what might be painted there next by God's hand. And if he has changed his mind and is following us, we're not going to have an easy time of it! Now," he concluded, "I've done the list as you asked me to. It's your turn. The whole of the truth--you promised!"

"All right, Moses agreed. "In a nut shell, it's this. I'm not worried about Pharaoh, even though I entirely agree with your analysis of his character, blindspots and probable actions. Yahweh can counter anything Pharaoh can throw at us without even making an effort. He is God, after all. So that's no problem."

"But how? What will we do? What will He do?"

Aaron had allowed a fraction of his anxiety to emerge in his rapid questions, and his tone stopped Moses in his tracks. He grasped his brother by one shoulder and wheeled him around so they stood fact to face. "Look at me!" he commanded, and Aaron, caught on the rising crest of his wave of terror, stopped with a gasp. He closed his mouth and did as Moses had ordered, staring into the younger man's eyes with such desperation that Moses all but looked away. "I'm sorry," he said after a moment. "Aaron, you should have told me. I didn't realize you were so frightened. Now look. When it comes time for us to do anything, the Lord will tell us exactly what it is we are to do. And He will defend us against anything Pharaoh has in mind. Until he tells us what to do, there's nothing we can do, or should be doing. Our job is to listen and wait--and meanwhile to keep our 600,000 men and their families moving behind Him, camping where He indicates, trusting in His care and praising His Name. That's all! All right?"

"All right," agreed Aaron more calmly. "You're right, of course. I'm sorry. I didn't mean--"

"Don't worry about it!" his brother interrupted. He smiled reassuringly but tightened his grip on Aaron's shoulders. He had more he had to say, if he were to keep his word to tell Aaron the whole truth, and he did not relish the prospect.

"But there is another factor," he began again, and felt Aaron grow suddenly still in his grip with that concentration of attention, energy, love and purpose that marked him when he brought his whole being to bear on someone else's difficulties. The sudden presence warmed Moses to the core of his being, and with an inner flush of unspoken grateful love, he went on more briskly. "I mean us. The Hebrews--sheep-dense, silly, stubborn, fearful,--sons of Israel and children of the promise Yahweh made to Abraham. We are the only real problem we have."

"You keep on saying so, and obviously you believe it and it worries you a lot," said Aaron with a puzzled frown, "but, I'm sorry, Moses, I just don't see it. I hate to add to your burden, but why?"

"Well," his brother replied. "Yahweh can do anything for us, and anything against anyone who dares to oppress us, but he can't make us be faithful to Him.

He can demand our obedience, but we are the ones who decide whether to obey--or not. In the same way, He can't make us trust Him or love Him. He can give us gifts--but He can't make us take them. He can ask us to do all these things--but that's as far as He can go."

"Like love between a wife and her husband?" suggested Aaron. "The wife is given to her husband in marriage, but whether she loves him or not is entirely within her control. Either he wins her trust and love, or he fails to win them--and there's no way he can control the outcome."

"That's it," his brother approved. "It's a strange way for God to act, but in a way it proves Yahweh is the only God there is or can be."

"How so?" Aaron frowned his puzzlement.

"Because," Moses explained, "only God would dare, could afford, to let creatures be that free. You noticed, no doubt, that the priests of Ra rule the Egyptians by force and fear, whether the people like it or not. They have to. If people decided not to worship Ra, he would disappear, and so would his priests. They, the ones supposed to be closest to the sun-god, don't trust him to be able to stand up for himself and deal with those who defy him, so they take very good care that the people are kept terrified of the possible consequences of defying Ra that they don't even think of it as a possibility. Yahweh doesn't even have a priesthood--and He takes care of His own defense very nicely, thank you!"

"So that's why you had me recite the ten plagues!" exclaimed Aaron. "You were right! I did need to be reminded of that crucial difference between Yahweh and all other gods!"

"Think again!" Moses reminded him, but the younger man was not smiling. "I told you *I* needed to hear the wonders, and I meant it. I did."

"Why?" asked Aaron.

"Because--well, because I got so worried about our weakness--"

"Wait a minute!" Aaron interrupted. "You just got

finished saying Yahweh can do anything, and I just
got finished repeating the ten things He did to make
Pharaoh let us go. What weakness of ours can negate
that power?"

"I told you!" his brother snapped. "Our freedom to
choose to love and trust Him--or not to. All 600,000 of us
men, and our wives and children, have to make that
choice and stick to it, even when Pharaoh's army
shows up to take us back to Egypt!"

There was a pause. Then Aaron said, very quietly
but very distinctly, "You said 'when Pharaoh's army
shows up.' Don't you mean 'if?'"

"No more than you should," replied Moses, the edge
not quite gone from his voice. "You've just spent a half
hour proving conclusively that Pharaoh has to try to get
us back. Weren't you listening?" Then, more gently, he
went on, "Of course he will come, and with his whole
army. And they will be riding in chariots. We're on
foot, and we have women, children and all the beasts
with us. So even with three days start they're bound to
catch up with us."

"Especially since, on the course we're following now,
we're doubling back on our tracks. Moses, why didn't
we take the direct northern route through Philistine
territory? It would have been quicker than this."

"Three guesses--the first two don't count," replied
his brother, somewhat grimly. "The Philistines
wouldn't have let us pass without a fight,and they
probably would have liked 600,000 men for slaves, to say
nothing of the women and children, and our Egyptian
gold and silver and our herds. And, as Yahweh put it
to me, if our ex-slaves saw they were going to have to
fight to keep the freedom He had given them, they
would very likely have turned around and gone back to
Egypt. That's why He routed us south along the desert
road."

"That makes sense," Aaron nodded. "But why did
we turn back this morning and head north again? And
where are we to camp? It's close to sundown and even
with the Cloud become Fire, our people don't really like

night travel."

"The Lord told me to encamp before Pi-hahiroth between Migdol and the sea, in front of Baal-zephon."

"And just how are we supposed to do that!"
demanded a cutting voice just behind the brothers.

Moses jumped involuntarily but Aaron turned slowly
and said in a provoking, deliberately sweet tone, "Why
Sister Dear! How nice for all of us that you have so fully
recovered your usual self-command and charm! What
can we do for you?"

In spite of himself Moses grinned. Aaron was a
good choice for a spokesman in a tight spot, whether
the adversary was Pharaoh or Miriam. He resolved to
stay out from the flashing verbal daggers of these
experienced opponents and wrapped himself in studied silence, eyes fixed on the Cloud. Let Aaron deal with
Miriam; he must commune with the Lord.

The certainty that they had arrived at the Lord's
chosen campsite came upon him just as the sun was
about to set.

"We are here!" he announced, his voice quelling the
demanding brass of Miriam's mezzo and the shining
silver of Aaron's deliberately drawling tenor with the
finality of a huge drum.

Miriam looked around. She saw in front of her the
sea, its reeds tall and close set. Then turning, she looked directly northwest. Her mouth dropped and she
drew in a deep breath. But instead of the shattering
scream which Aaron knew, from painful experience,
she was capable of delivering, Miriam simply reached
behind her for Aaron, found his hand and whispered,
"Look!"

She pointed and Aaron's eyes followed her finger.
He saw a cloud of dust in the distance, and then, on the
breeze, heard the unmistakable jingle of metal and
tramp of horses.

"It is the army of the Pharaoh," said Moses, his voice
still carrying the solemn drumbeat with which he had
announced their camp site.

"So he is supposed to be here?" asked Miriam in a

steady, even voice in which neither fear nor anger had any place. At her question Moses blinked but silenced his surprise with no other outward sign of his amazement at this side of Miriam which he had not so far seen. "Yes, he is," he said adopting her dispassionate tone. "The Lord said that, once we had turned back to camp here, he would pursue us, thinking the desert had closed in on us and left us wandering."

"With the sea in front of us, there's nowhere to run to, even if we could outrun chariots," Miriam responded in the same cool, judicial tone which was as new to Aaron's experience of her as it was to Moses, "and the Egyptians are closing in rapidly. Yahweh certainly doesn't make things easy on Himself!"

"That He doesn't," Aaron agreed. "You don't sound worried, though, Miriam."

"Of course not! Yahweh is God, remember!" She smiled at Aaron with a triumph that had nothing to do with their present duel and, indeed, nothing personal in it. "Why should I worry?" she asked rhetorically. "I don't see how He's going to handle this--but that's not my problem! He will, one way or another!"

Moses, meeting her eyes, smiled and was about to reply when a shout rose from the following Israelites, and, as if catapulted from their midst, a knot of five men, all bellowing at the top of their lungs, landed in a heap at Moses' feet.

"One at a time!" commanded Moses in the drum voice, and, one at a time, the five spoke, or shrieked their terror and rage.

"Were there no burial places in Egypt, that you had to bring us out here to die in the desert?"

"Why did you do this to us?"

"Why did you bring us out of Egypt?"

"Did we not tell you this when we said 'Leave us alone. Let us serve the Egyptians'?"

"Far better for us to be the slaves of the Egyptians than to die in the desert!"

"Fear not!" The voice of Moses cut through the rising hysteria of the Israelites, as a single soaring trumpet note blares golden against an orchestral storm. In this case what followed was not harmonic resolution, but a ragged silence like a jagged, pulsing wound. Without a pause Moses continued, the trumpet of his voice deepened and sustained by the steady drum beat of triumphant certainty which had marked every command he had given them from God. "Stand your ground, and you will see the victory the Lord will win for you today," he promised them. "The Egyptians whom you see today you will never see again. The Lord Himself will fight for you; you have only to keep still."

At that point the sun dropped below the horizon and the light faded rapidly. As it did, the familiar stars came out with a rush, but the Cloud, instead of igniting with its usual internal Fire, grew black and shifted position to the rear of the group, so that it encircled the 600,000 men, with their women, children and beasts, and interposed itself between the Israelites and the oncoming forces.

Aaron was stunned. The materialization of his fears in the sight of the oncoming Egyptians, and the expression of them in the terrors of the five hysterical spokesmen of the people, the force of the presence of Yahweh made manifest in his brother's speech and the rapidity with which the Cloud had become their shield and the people had begun to make camp, their fears miraculously put to rest, left him silent and dazed. At last he looked toward Moses, but his brother was communing with Yahweh, as was evident from his withdrawal inward and his concentrated, exalted and peaceful expression.

Unable to make contact with Moses, he turned to Miriam, but his usually volatile sister had, it seemed, nothing to say, and so she said nothing, contenting herself with staring at Moses, her mouth slightly open, but with no hint of fear or hostility in her bearing.

Aaron was alone in this new darkness, and he was afraid. It appeared to him that he was the only who was afraid, and this added isolation triggered a panic within him. What should he do? What could he do? He was all alone with both Moses and Miriam out of reach, and 600,000 men, with women, children and beasts, his people, Aaron's people, not Moses-the-latecomer's people, peacefully setting up camp in the teeth of a rapidly advancing enemy! Suppose the Egyptians came through the Cloud? They would decimate the Israelites at will, or simply round them up and bring them back to slavery in Egypt, and the silly sheep would turn around and go peacefully back, to slaughter or slow death. He had to do something! He had to!

But there was nothing to be done. That was the trouble with having a volunteer God, thought Aaron somewhat bitterly. He didn't exist because the people needed Him to; He wasn't their god because they made Him their god; He did not need their honor, their sacrifice, their worship. They needed Him--and they had no "leverage" in dealing with Him. He had chosen them to be His people, and had chosen to be their God through His choosing of Abraham and his descendents, because He wanted to, and only the compulsion of His will kept Him choosing them. They could no nothing to ensure His fidelity, to guarantee their own safety or their position as His people. Priests of Ra, fulfilling their ritual, could see to it that Ra stayed friendly to Egypt, on Egypt's side in any war, could guarantee Ra's protection. But with Yahweh, no sacrifice or deed the Israelites had within their power to do could move Him so much as a hairsbreadth in any direction He had not chosen to go. They were His, and they were power-less. Powerless!

The scream of terror and despair in Aaron had gotten to his back teeth, and he clenched them hard to prevent its escape. Whatever happened, whatever he had to do or say, he must not panic, must not cause a riot among the 600,000 and their dependents. If they had to go back to Egypt, and he could see no other result of the coming encounter, then let them go peacefully and save their lives. Living in the safety of slavery was surely better than being slaughtered for a chimerical freedom they would never taste?

"Aaron!"

At the sound of his name spoken, in that same golden trumpet tone Moses had used to calm the crowd, but so softly that only Aaron could hear it, the man jumped and wheeled toward the speaker. "Moses?" he implored, and the anguish in his soul invested his tone with the piercing pain of a dagger thrust.

"Aaron, you must not fail Yahweh!" Moses commanded. "You must trust Him. I need you to! I know what I am to do, but I need you, you and Miriam," he added and extended his arms to them, "both of you together, to help me."

Miriam stepped forward at once. "What can we do, brother? Moses, tell us--what can we do?" Her voice was firm and sweet, now, a cello singing a quiet affirmation. She half-turned and, her right hand grasping Moses left hand, extended her left to Aaron. He came forward slowly, still gripped by his terror and despair and leaning forward together his brother and sister each caught hold of one of his dangling damp hands. They pulled him toward them, their life and the certainty of their trust in Yahweh coursing through him. like two waves of fire. When the waves met at his heart, he was flooded with a sudden peace. He had not shared in the sudden transformation of the wounded silence of the camp to healed peace when Moses had spoken, but for him as well, wholeness had now been restored.

The night was still dark. He did not know how Yahweh would provide, but that He would was as solid and warmingly clear as the love of his brother and sister which cradled him now. Silently he wept, and did not trouble to hide the tears.

Then Moses moved from them to execute Yahweh's last orders. He turned to the sea and raised his staff, extending his hand over the sea. A strong east wind rose, flowing over the sea toward him. Hand in hand, Aaron and Miriam stood behind him, and felt with him the steady wind. In the moonlight the three saw what Yahweh was doing. A clear path was appearing straight through the center of the sea, extending from its farther shore to where they were standing. The waters were piled up on either side of this strip of dry land like a pair of walls.

"Rouse the people," Moses said to Aaron when the path at last was complete and dry. "We must move on."

Aaron obeyed. The 600,000 men, with their women, children and beasts, assembled in their somewhat casual line of march and began to walk past Moses who had his staff still raised and his hand extended over the sea. Dryshod, all 600,000 with their families and cattle, followed by their leader Moses with his brother Aaron and his sister Miriam, crossed safely to the other side of the sea.

Then Moses turned to look back on the path that had brought them to safety. It was just before dawn, and in the swiftly growing light he saw at the further end, Egyptian horses, chariots and charioteers, the Pharaoh's entire force, in fact, heading out after them across the sea. As the troops reached the mid-point of the sea the Lord, once again appearing as the Pillar of Fire, cast a glance upon the Egyptian force that threw it into a panic, and He so clogged their chariot wheels in the sandy sea bottom that they could hardly drive. With that, the Egyptians sounded retreat. It was plain to them that the same God that had sent ten horrendous plagues upon them and their stubborn Pharaoh to free this wretched slave-people He had, for some reason known only to Himself, chosen for His own, was now actively fighting on their behalf. This was no place for any Egyptian to be who wanted to die in his bed!

But the realization came too late. Moses had already obeyed Yahweh's command: "Stretch out your hand over the sea, that the waters may flow back upon the Egyptians, upon their chariots and their charioteers."

As the dawn blazed into day, the waters of the sea flowed back to their normal depth and drowned the entire Egyptian army. No one escaped.

Seeing the total destruction of their enemy in the sea, which had opened to let them pass through and now protected them from further pursuit, all Israel, with one voice, joined Moses in a solemn song of praise of Yahweh. Then, with the Cloud again at their head, they moved forward steadily into the unknown, walking in trust to the land of promise.

The Centurion's Servant

"How is he?" The questioner, a man in his early fifties, stood automatically erect, his posture, like his expression, disciplined by years of service in Rome's legions. His service had been hard, most of it on the Empire's shifting frontiers, and military discipline had saved his position, his men and his own life more often than he was comfortable remembering.

Now, waiting for the surgeon's response, Junius stood perfectly still--contained, at ease within himself, in command of his world. No one but Agrippa, his friend since both had been recruits in the same century commanded by old Severus, could have guessed his anxiety.

Agrippa exhaled sharply through his nose, narrowing his eyes and pressing his lips together in an unconscious expression of anger. Junius knew the look and sound well. It was the outward sign of a loss of some kind in the unending war against death that Agrippa had been waging for as long as Junius had known him. Invisibly, Junius flinched. "Not now, not this one, gods!--not Marcus! Not my sister's only son!" The muscles at his jaw hinges jumped with the force of his demand and the greater force required not to let that demand be guessed by any save the gods who read the heart.

Finally Agrippa looked up from Marcus, a slender eleven-year-old, his child's body struggling for breath against the paralysis that was slowly immobilizing his diaphragm and chest muscles. Agrippa shook his head once, pulling the corners of his mouth in even further for an instant. "Not good," he said flatly. "Not good."

Junius, braced for this, nodded, then asked, "Any hope?"

The question was uncharacteristic both in words and

in the unguarded plea that rang in them. Sharply, Agrippa looked into his friend's eyes for an instant. Seeing the pain there, he was silent for a moment. Then he deliberately took hold of Junius' right shoulder with a firm left hand. "No. None at all," he said gently.

Junius released the breath he didn't know he had been holding, and, feeling tears prickling behind his eyelids and forming a swollen lump in this throat, turned partly away. When he again had command of himself, he turned back to Agrippa and said simply, "I was afraid of that. I knew, really, but hearing you say it..." his gray eyes sought the physician's dark brown ones as his voice trailed off. After a long moment, he asked, "Agrippa, what can I do for him? What can we do? What can be done. If anything," he added.

"Nothing that will heal him," said Agrippa bluntly. He knew Junius preferred clarity when a crisis was at hand, and that the grizzled centurion would count vaguely soothing generalities the work of an enemy, not the comfort of a friend.

"But anything, anything that might make this-- passage, this dying, easier?" Junius' insistence while it derived some added intensity from his affection for his nephew, his dead sister Gloria's only child and her very image with straight dark hair and dark blue eyes, was characteristic of the commander. One of the bonds between Junius and Agrippa was the gift each had for keeping sight of each of the individuals in his charge, even while he planned for, and dealt with, the century as a unit in the war it was being used to fight. Junius took the injuries and the deaths of his men as person- ally as did Agrippa. For them, casualties were not statistics, but men with wives and families.

"Anything?" repeated Agrippa. "Well," he paused. Then, "Well, while he can swallow, we'll get meat broth into him. We'll continue with the hot wet com- presses on his neck, back and thighs and the warm baths; they seem to be relieving the muscle spasms. And we'll keep moving his arms and legs and chang- ing his position in bed. But once the paralysis immobilizes his breathing, he'll die. And," the physician's lips tightened and his voice became an angry rasp, "I don't know how to prevent it, or even make it easier. I just don't, Junius. And I don't know of anyone who does, even in Rome--or Egypt, which is more to the point." At Junius' slight questioning frown he added, "Mother Egypt is the source of medical knowledge, or at least Egyptian physicians have collected and organized all that men have so far learned about the body's diseases and their cures. This disease," he indicated Marcus, "is beyond them."

Junius slumped into his chair. He pushed aside the reports and maps which had accumulated there since Marcus' illness with his left hand and leaned forward, resting his left elbow in the cleared space and his forehead on a supporting left hand. He began to drum on the table with his right hand, softly but insistently. Marcus stirred at the sound and seemed to be trying to speak.

"What is it lad?" asked Agrippa, bending over him and wiping his damp forehead with a cool cloth.

"Uncle," the boy whispered, and Junius was on his feet at once and to the boy's bed it two swift steps.

"Yes, Marcus. I'm here," said Junius in a steady voice. "What is it?"

"...thirsty," said the boy, and Junius looked up to find Agrippa across the bed from him with a cup in one hand and a linen dressing in the other. "Dip the dressing into the broth," Agrippa instructed him, "and put it against his lips. Squeeze it gently as he sucks, and, when it's dry, soak up some more from the cup. The more of it he can take, the better. I'll change the compresses."

As Junius was feeding Marcus, he heard a sound behind him. He turned his head sharply and saw Jacob and his younger brother Benjamin standing by the tent flap staring at Marcus, who was accustomed to play with them when he was "off duty." His role as a junior orderly, while it was not an official rank, and had no place either in the Legion's bookkeeping or on the Century's troop roster, had become a real set of responsibilities in Junius' handling of it, and Marcus' day and week followed, though in modified form, the century's patterns. Now Marcus' two friends looked at each other in dismay. "Please, sir," said Jacob, who was within a month of Marcus' age but seemed, because of his smaller stature, to be younger, "can we talk to Marcus?"

"He's very sick, Jacob," replied Junius who knew, as a matter of course, the names and family connections not only of all his men but of all their civilian friends and contacts. "I'm not sure he'll recognize you."

"Please, sir," echoed Benjamin, and then added, "It's very important sir. It's about Jesus. He's here in Capernaum and--"

"Hush, Ben! We have to tell Marcus first. Then he has to report to his un--to Centurion Junius. That's the way the Legion works," Jacob instructed his younger brother. He looked at Junius. "Isn't that ri--correct, sir?" he asked.

The smile that warmed Junius' eyes and heart made no alteration in his voice nor in the military set of his mouth. He kept feeding Marcus, gently squeezing soup from the linen dressing into the boy's mouth as Marcus sucked at it, while he answered seriously, "Yes, Jacob, that's the Legion's way. Marcus has taught you well. But in this case, I think we had better skip the middle stage; Marcus isn't up to it today. What about Jesus?"

The boys looked at each other for a moment. Then Jacob nodded. Benjamin, his tongue freed, rattled out at top speed, "Jesus! Jesus is wonderful, sir! He's the most--He does everything! He makes blind people see and deaf people hear! He talks to children--He likes us! He makes lepers whole again! He drives devils out of people! And He makes crippled people able to walk again!"

"Yes, so I have heard," replied the centurion. "What of it?"

"Oh, Sir! We wanted Marcus to come with us to Jesus so Jesus could make him better!" exploded Ben.

"Jesus is back in Capernaum, sir," said Jacob more

slowly. "Do you think Marcus could come with us to see him? Because if he could, I know Jesus would make him better." The older boy's steady dark eyes met and held the centurion's grey gaze with a look that was part sorrow, part plea and part hope. He waited.

Junius returned the look for a long moment. Involuntarily his eyes shifted to the slight figure on the bed, and Jacob's eyes followed his. Though Marcus continued to suck at the linen dressing, drawing broth from it eagerly, the boy was having increasing difficulty in breathing. He fought to draw the steamy air into his lungs, then had to struggle equally hard to expel it again. It was clear he was weakening.

"No Jacob, he can't! Use your head! Don't come here bothering Ju--the Centurion any more with such nonsense!" Agrippa's voice, which cracked like a whiplash in the silent tent, raised a flush on Jacob's cheeks. He bit his lower lip and dropped his eyes to the ground. "I didn't mean," he began but Benjamin interrupted with his usual impetuous frankness.

"Sir, we weren't bothering the centurion! If we were, he'd tell us so himself! And we're right! Jesus can make Marcus better when we bring him there! You can't do that--you've tried! Why can't Marcus go to Jesus!"

"Ben!" Jacob, horrified at his younger brother's boldness in speaking to the physician, tried to silence the boy and apologize to the elders at the same time. He was forestalled by Junius.

The centurion raised his hand to calm Agrippa whose wrath (never far from the surface when he was losing a patient and had exhausted all his resources of healing), had kindled at the anger in Ben's voice and was about to blaze out. Meeting Junius' eyes, the physician caught his breath, clamped his tongue between his teeth and turned his back roughly on Ben, to continue changing the hot, wet compresses on Marcus' thighs and lower trunk.

Then Junius said quietly, "I'm sure you're right Ben. I've heard many wonderful things about Jesus, and I know He is kind to children. But I'm afraid it's too late. Agrippa has done all any physician could have done for him." Putting down the cup of broth, Junius reached for the physician's hand and held it in a warm grip for a moment then released it. "All anyone could have done," he repeated with gentle emphasis, "but Marcus can no longer breathe easily--you hear. The disease has won."

Both boys nodded, and tears filled Ben's eyes. Jacob asked in a small voice, "Then Marcus is dying?" At the centurion's reluctant nod the boy's shoulders drooped. "Then, sir, the physician was right. We are bothering you. We're sorry, sir. We didn't mean to. We hoped we could help."

The boy's voice deserted him at that, and blindly he put out his hand for Ben to lead him away.

"You did help," Junius assured him, his voice strong and confident. "You've given me an idea!"

The three stared at him, the boys with dawning hope and Agrippa with consternation. "Now Junius," began the physician in a warning tone, "he can't be moved unless you want to kill him at once!"

"I don't propose to move him," explained the centurion, "only to bring him to Jesus' attention. If He knows--"

"He'll cure him!" interrupted Ben in a joyful shout. "I'm sorry, sir," he corrected himself in a whisper as Jacob's hand came down on his shoulder. "But we will! We'll run and tell him! And if Father and Uncle Reuben would come with us, we could get through the crowd really fast! Everybody gets out of the way for them," he explained proudly to Junius.

"That's because they're leaders in the synagogue, Ben!" said Jacob, a touch of impatience sharpening the edges of his usually calm voice as the shadow of a frown darkened his eyes. This one would be dangerous if roused, Agrippa commented to himself, and turned back to his work. As long as Marcus was not moved in this hare-brained scheme, he didn't mind what they planned. It was not his concern.

It was Junius' concern, however, and even as his hands resumed their work of getting broth into Marcus, he was planning strategy. "Yes," he said to Jacob and Ben, "if your father and your uncle would do me that favor, I would be most grateful. If Jesus will heal Marcus..." his voice trailed away.

"Let's go Jacob!" urged the impatient Ben. "We've got to hurry! Listen to how Marcus is breathing! And you know how slow Uncle Reuben can be! Come on!" He swung to the tent entrance, tugging at Jacob's hand as he turned.

But the older boy, used to countering his younger brother's impetuosity, planted his feet and did not move. "May we go, sir?" he asked Junius formally, and the centurion, recalled to the present with a start, nodded at once. "Yes, by all means Jacob, Benjamin. Go. And thank you!" he called after their rapidly re-treating backs.

When approached by his sons with the centurion's request Judah, was delighted. "He has been so good to us," he urged Reuben, "that we ought to do what he asked even if it were really impossible. And this is nothing."

"It's everything to him," Reuben corrected him, "but yes, we must go."

"Now, uncle, now!" urged Ben, to whom even this brief exchange had seemed to take an uncountable age.

"All rash haste leads certainly to poverty, nephew!" intoned Reuben. Ben closed his mouth.

"Uncle," said Jacob respectfully, but with an urgency even greater than Benjamin's, "that is true, but this haste does not seem rash to me. Marcus is dying now! He can scarcely breathe! If we don't hurry, we may be too late." He paused, expectantly.

The men exchanged glances. Then Judah said decisively, "We will come. And we will bring Jesus to the Centurion's quarters."

As Ben had boasted, the crowds did part for Judah and Reuben as they made their purposeful way toward its center where Jesus was. "See?" whispered Ben to

Jacob as the two shadowed their elders, but was silenced by the older boy with a firm hand.

"Teacher," Judah began when he was face to face with Jesus, "we have a favor to ask of You."

Jesus looked inquiringly from Judah to Reuben and back. Then, his eye caught by a movement slightly to the elders' left, he glanced down. Seeing the hovering Benjamin with Jacob just behind him, Jesus smiled a welcome, and the boys wriggled through the last of the crowd and ran to hug Him and be hugged in return.

Judah, watching the swift exchange, felt a warmth he had not known before. He was still smiling when Jesus looked directly at him, reminding him that he had urgent business with the strange man people were calling "Master," and "Son of Man" and even, in whispers, "Messiah." "Sir," he said quietly, "the Centurion here has a servant who is dying. He asked us to ask you to come and heal him."

"He deserves the favor," interjected Reuben. "He loves our people and even built our synagogue for us."

Jesus looked at the men for a long moment, then down at the boys whose eyes pleaded with Him as they held their breath. Then, "I will come and cure him," He replied.

Jacob and Benjamin with a single shout hugged Jesus again and tore through the crowd. They raced to the Centurion's quarters in record time and began to shout, "He's coming! He's coming! He's coming!" as they skidded up to the door which Agripped opened at once. "Jesus is coming!" said Ben abruptly dropping his voice.

Junius turned slightly from the bed where Marcus still struggled for breath. "Coming?" he asked sharply, but in a tone kept low. "Here? To me?"

"Yes, sir!" said the boys in a joyful whisper.

"No!" said the Centurion so emphatically that everyone jumped. "He come here? That must not be. He must not trouble Himself. I am not worthy to have Him enter my house. Tell Him so. Say that is why I did not presume to go to Him myself. Tell Him all He

has to do is give an order and Marcus," his eyes clung
to the dying boy, and his voice broke with unshed tears,
"will be healed," he finished.   "After all," he added to
Jacob, "I am a man who knows the meaning of an
order! I have soldiers under my command. I say to
one. 'On your way!' and off he goes, to another, 'Come
here!' and he comes, and to my slave, 'Do this!, and he
does it."

Jacob drew himself erect. "Yes, sir," he said. Then
in a formal tone he asked, "May I go sir?" At Junius'
nod, he stood very straight, said "Thank you, sir" and
gave Junius the salute the Legion members were
accustomed to use on leaving their commander to
execute an order.

Junius returned the salute automatically, then
looked at Jacob in open-mouthed astonishment.
"What--?" he began. But the boy had already gathered
his brother and left the centurion's quarters on the
run, headed back to Jesus to deliver Junius' message to
him. This time breaking through the crowd was easier,
and almost at once Jacob found himself out of breath in
front of Jesus. "No! Stop!" he said holding up both
hands and shaking his head. He could not for the
moment say more, but stood gasping for breath.

Jesus stopped at once, waiting until Jacob had gotten
his breath and could explain. Judah was less patient.
"Son!" he said sternly, "This is no time to play foolish
games!"

"I'm not, sir," Jacob replied. Then, his breathing
growing easier he said to Jesus, "The Centurion says to
say to you, 'Sir, do not trouble Yourself, for I am not
worthy to have You enter my house. That is why I did
not presume to come to You myself.'" He drew a deep
breath. "He said to say to You, 'Just give the order and
my servant will be healed.'"

Jesus said nothing. He looked intently at Jacob, His
eyebrows slightly raised and waited. The boy returned
the look, then, suddenly smiled. "He said," he went on
in the same conversational tone Junius had used, 'I,
too, am a man who knows the meaning of an order,

having soldiers under my command.'" The boy's voice unconsciously warmed on the last words and he straightened himself to military erectness. "'I say to one, "On you way!" and off he goes, to another, "Come here!" and he does it'" Then, the recitation complete, Jacob took the military "at ease" stance and waited, beaming expectantly at Jesus, Who smiled back. Benjamin, silent for once, simply stared at him, then he turned with the rest of the staring, buzzing crowd to look at Jesus.

Jesus turned from Jacob to the crowd. His eyes touched Reuben and Judah briefly and warmly, then drew in the entire throng. "I tell you," he said in that clear tone which was not loud but seemed to ring in the ears of the most distant listener, "I have never found so much faith among the Israelites!" The crowd stirred, but quieted as Jesus went on, "Mark what I say! Many will come from the east and the west, and will find a place at the banquet in the Kingdom of God with Abraham, Isaac and Jacob, while the natural heirs of the Kingdom will be driven out into the dark. Wailing will be heard there, and gnashing of teeth."

A darkness seemed to come over the day, and Benjamin shivered. But then Jesus was turning to him and Jacob with a smile that brought the sun blazing out, warming them both. Jacob asked confidently, his eyes alight, "Have you any orders for me, or any message for me to take to the Centurion?" He smiled.

Jesus, answering the smile, nodded. "Go home. It shall be done because you trusted," He said.

Jacob saluted. "Yes, sir!" he said with trumpets in his voice, and wheeling ran back to the Centurion's quarters with Benjamin at his heels.

This time it was not Agrippa who flung open the door but Junius, wreathed in smiles. His arm was around Marcus who stood next to him in the full bloom of radiant health, just in front of Agrippa who was still wiping his eyes on a linen compress.

"Sir! Marcus!" shouted the boys as they slid to a stop.

"Marcus! You're well! You're all well! Jesus made you well!" shouted Ben, and at Marcus' sudden blank look, Junius intervened.

"We'll tell him the whole story inside," he said quietly. "It'll take some telling, I think, and we'll all want to hear all of it." Agrippa nodded vigorously, and Jacob caught his eye and smiled shyly at him.

"Thank you, lad," said the physician simply and, moving to Jacob hugged him.

"Perhaps you'd better say 'soldier'" suggested Junius mildly and, as Jacob turned to him in wonder, hope and delight battling for expression on his face, the centurion smiled. "You have done an excellent day's work today, Jacob!" he said warmly. Then, with quiet dignity he faced Jacob and said formally, "Good work, soldier! Welcome to the Century! Welcome to the Legion."

Every movement exact, Junius gave Jacob the Legion's salute and the young man reverently returned it. For a long moment their eyes held. Then, simultaneously, they smiled and turned together to enter the centurion's quarters, drawing Marcus, Agrippa and Benjamin in with them.

The Paralyzed Man

"But why not, if He can heal you? Surely it's worth that much of a risk! All He can do is say no!" The speaker was Jonathan, a vigorous young fisherman with a shock of dark hair that wouldn't stay in place under any conditions, but seemed to reflect in its unruliness his own volatile temperament. Now it stood in spiky tufts, emphasizing his exasperation with Judah, his dearest friend.

Judah, too, had been a fisherman, but an unlucky fall had left him paralyzed. Now, instead of living the active, fruitful life he and his beloved Ruth had planned, he lay, day and night, on his mat, relying on family and friends to supply his every need. Physicians had told him he would never fish again, never walk again, never again be able to live independently, and the diagnosis had broken his spirit.

Now he looked at his friend dully. "Why bother Him?" he wanted to know. "There's nothing He can do--and even if He could, why should He do it for me? I'm no one. He's never heard of me. Why should He care?"

"I've just told you!" exploded Jonathan. "He's not like that! You don't have to be anybody for Him to help you! All you have to do is come to Him and ask! He cures everybody--anybody! Nobody pays Him anything, either, and He's back here in Capernaum--just got in this morning! I tell you, Judah, it's your chance!"

"Nice of you not to say my only chance," remarked Judah. "It is, you know."

"Then why won't you take it!" demanded Jonathan. "Anyone'd think you liked being this way--you're so balky about even trying this Jesus!"

"Like it!" The thrust had gone home, rousing Judah from his lethargy and tapping the well of anger and bitterness that had been filling in the handsome fisherman.

"Like it!" he repeated. "Like lying here in my own sweat, waiting for someone to bathe me, change my tunic, feed me, wipe my eyes, brush a fly off me? Like thinking all the time, remembering what I was, what I planned, what I wanted--still want, except I can't ever have it? Like being this way? Guess again!" He paused for breath.

"Then why--"began Jonathan, but Judah cut him off.

"Why? Why my almost-was brother-in-law? Because not hoping when there is no hope, and can be no hope, is easier than hoping--crawling up out of Gehenna when you're going to be shoved right back down into the fire again. Not hoping is smart. Hoping is dumb--a fool's game or a child's fantasy, and I'm neither a fool or a child."

Jonathan was silent, considering the rage of his friend dispassionately, as he automatically reached for the linen cloth, dipped it in the bowl of cool herb-scented water and, squeezing it out, wiped the sweat and tears from Judah's face, which twisted into a bitter grimace under his friend's hands. "Then," Jonathan said at last in a thoughtful tone, "you think my sister Ruth is a fool? Or a fantasizing child? I thought you loved her."

"What has Ruth got to do with this?" snapped Judah.

"Besides being my only sister and best friend, and besides being your betrothed wife you mean?" asked Jonathan in the same thoughtful tone. "Well, for one thing, she sent an answer to your question which I'm supposed to deliver to you just as you told me to deliver yours to her--without change, omission, addition or comment of any kind. I never met two more--well, never mind!"

"What did she say? She did agree with me, didn't she? She did agree to break off the betrothal?" Judah's speech rushed at Jonathan like a thrown spear.

Jonathan opened his mouth to reply, but Judah broke in and Jonathan closed his mouth again. "Of course, she did," declared Judah. "She's neither a fool nor a child. She had to. She couldn't do anything else. She can't do anything else."

Then, as Jonathan again opened his mouth to speak, Judah interrupted, impatiently, "Well? What did she say? Jonathan! What did she say?"

Jonathan once again opened his mouth to reply, but Judah again cut in. "Oh, I know! You don't have to tell me". But what did she say? Jonathan! What did she say?"

After a pause, Jonathan asked judiciously, "You sure you're finished? I wouldn't want to interrupt you!"

"I'm finished!" said Judah, and then, with a rueful laugh, repeated, "I'm finished! Sorry Jonathan! I'll listen. What did Ruth say?"

"Ruth said," reported her brother, "that the only way you'll get rid of her is to hand her a bill of divorce that you've written out with your own hands. She says she won't accept it if you ask anyone to hand it to her for you, or if you have any scribe write it for you. Then she said..."

"But I can't do that!" Judah was indignant. "I can't use my hands! She knows that!"

"She said," repeated Jonathan, and Judah subsided, with an apologetic mumble "She said that there were two reasons why the bill of divorce ought to be unacceptable to you, and that you ought to be able to figure both of them out, if you would stop wallowing in self-pity and use your brains for thinking, instead of pretending they're chopped liver! That," he added with one eyebrow cocked at Judah and a slight smile, "is a direct quotation."

"I recognized the style!" said Judah. He shook his head and smiled in his turn. "Your sister is a determined woman!"

"She gets it from her betrothed husband," answered Jonathan. "Anyway, she said if you didn't instantly think of the first reason--the hands she listed as second, by the way, but she told me you'd put them first--you should remember back to Passover last year and your declaration about Aunt Miriam and Uncle Joachim and their fight about Hannah.

Jonathan paused. Judah frowned for a moment, then said, "All I remember saying was that Uncle Joachim was right--that the only possible ground for divorce is infidelity, and that if Hannah wanted Jacob to divorce her, she was asking to be called an adulteress, and that if Aunt Miriam wanted her daughter and his to be judged a whore by all Capernaum, he didn't and would do all he could to prevent it!"

"You agreed with Uncle Joachim," repeated Jonathan, in a tone halfway between a question and a statement.

"Yes, of course," said Judah. "But this is different! Everyone knows--"

"Nothing," Jonathan cut in swiftly, "except that you believe, and have publicly declared, that infidelity is the only ground for a divorce, and that you are divorcing my sister! That means, my dear brother-in-law, you are legally giving my sister the name and reputation of infidelity--and what honorable man will marry a woman publicly and formally declared unfaithful--a whore, if you like?"

"But bethrothal..."

"Counts as marriage among us, remember?"

"But we never--"

"Doesn't matter and you know it!" Jonathan declared triumphantly. "She's got you, you know! For if you will not dishonor her, you must take her into your home and you will not dishonor her."

Judah shook his head wonderingly. "What a woman!" he said reverently. "What an amazing--what a wonderful--what a woman!" He looked up at Jonathan, who was regarding him with a mix of amusement, compassion and genuine regard. "And I couldn't ask for a better brother-in-law, or a truer friend," he said. "But about this Jesus business..."

"Ah, Judah?" said Jonathan in the tone reserved for telling an opponent he has just moved from check to mate while thinking he was avoiding a trap three moves away. "This 'Jesus business', as you call it is

Ruth's idea."

Judah was stunned. "Ruth's!"

"Yes, Ruth's! She has it all figured out. We carry you on your mat to Jesus, He heals you and--we all dance together at your wedding!"

"But--"

"Ruth loves you, Judah. As you are, she loves you, and she is determined to be married to you, and to stay married to you, until one of you dies. As you are! But because she loves you, as you are, she knows you'll be happier up and around, working and supporting her and your ten children..."

"Ten!"

"Ten! Don't interrupt! Than you will be having her take care of you. She has it all planned--and my advice to you," said Jonathan with a grin, "is to keep still and let her do it her way! After the long and varied experience of a lifetime as her younger brother, I can assure you, that is the only way to survive!"

Judah smiled. But after Jonathan had left, promising to return with Saul, his and Ruth's elder brother, and Abner and Joseph, their cousins, Hannah's brothers, Judah relapsed into the lethargic gloom that had been dragging at his spirit for weeks. It was all very well for Ruth to engineer this, this meeting, and fine for her brothers and cousins to march along cheerfully carrying him like a sack of wool to this Jesus--but then?

"I have no claims on Him," Judah told himself. "I don't even believe He can cure me. They say I have nothing to lose, but I do. If Jesus can cure me, it is because He comes from God, for only God can heal a man paralyzed by an injury like mine. But, then, if I go to Him, I go as I am--but if Jesus is from God He will know me, all of me, as I really am, and no man can dare face God that way. Then, to go to Him and think 'Well, if You can, do it' that would be an insult. That is what we Israelites did all the way from Egypt to the Promised Land--at the Red Sea, with the manna, with the quail, with the water from the Rock, every time, the same insult. And here I am proposing to do the same thing: 'Heal me, and I'll say You're God's-- because I don't believe You can.' It would serve me right if He struck me dead on the spot. But I do want to be healed--and to be Ruth's husband, and to father and support the ten children--ten! What a woman!--and if He can do that--but I can't go to Him and pretend I believe He can when I don't--either way, it's a lie, and if He's God He'll be angry--and He'll be right to be."

These contradictory and troubling thoughts rolling on in a continuous chattering stream, interrupting each other and drowning each other out, eventually sent Judah into a troubled sleep. He did not hear Jonathan and Saul when they arrived with Ruth. Nor did he waken when, under Ruth's generalship, Abner and Joseph, on coming to the door were assigned the foot of his mat while Saul and Jonathan managed the head. The brief journey to the house of Ezra did not rouse him, nor did the gathering crowd which had packed the area around the house where Jesus was teaching and disputing with the Pharisees.

It was not until they put his mat down, placing it carefully on a level surface, that he began to emerge from his sleep. He was not quite sure whether he was awakening or whether the dreams had simply become a little more solid, more real if not more realistic.

He thought he heard Jonathan telling someone, "Three will do it," and heard that someone (Abner?), reply, "No, better make it four, or five to be safe. We don't want to dump him, after all, and we'll have to work from up here."

There was an odd, scrambling sound as though large, if not very heavy, flat things were being moved out of a fixed position and put to one side. Then a voice came from the left. It sounded like Saul, but what it was saying was more like a dream code than sense. "I've got them! I borrowed them from Benjamin. Three twenty-foot lengths of their heaviest stock." Benjamin, as far as Judah knew, was a scholar of the Law; perhaps there was another? Or perhaps the dream had given Benjamin a new occupation?

"Good! We'll use one here at the head, one in the middle and one at the end. When you have them secured, let me know. But hurry! We haven't got all day!" That was Jonathan again. Even in the dream, Judah reflected with a smile, Jonathan was the organizer. Now he was giving the rest of the dream's cast the remainder of their orders. "All secure? Good! Abner, you take the foot of the mat; Saul and Joseph, get on either side at the middle; I'll get at the head. Now, when I say 'Lift!' we all lift together, carry him to the hole and swing him through it, then lower him straight down, hand-over-hand, on the ropes. Got it?"

"Yes," replied a voice that sounded like Joseph's. "Are you sure we're in position?"

"Look for yourself!" snapped Abner. "It opens right over His head and in front of Him. He can't move because there are too many people--and nobody else can, either! They're too jammed in! I tell you it's perfect!"

"Are we ready, then?" asked Jonathan. "All right-- lift!"

At that Judah, who had been hazily observing this rather boring dream as a captive audience felt himself being swung in the air. As someone cautioned, "Careful! Don't drop him! He'll have enough to do without our throwing in a couple of broken bones!" Judah's eyes flew open. This dream was getting entirely too real!

What he saw made him blink rapidly and then catch his breath. There above him were blue sky and clouds, not the familiar ceiling of his house whose every crack he had long since memorized. And then, as he felt the mat being lowered, he realized that the odd knot about a foot above his nose was the closure of a kind of sling around his mat, that there was another at the same height above his stomach and that there was a third over his ankles. He saw swim past him the con-centrated faces of Joseph and Saul, at his mid-region and Abner frowning at his feet and then saw the exposed edge of a hole which seemed to be rimmed with roof tiles. As the hole and the peering faces of his straining friends receded from him, he understood that he was awake, not dreaming and was being lowered by three ropes through somebody's roof, but the reason for the maneuver was slower to come to him.

It wasn't until he had almost reach the ground that he remembered Ruth's determination that he be brought to Jesus for a cure. With that recollection the full force of the dilemma which he had left behind on entering his restless sleep returned, bringing with it undiluted horror. If he could have covered his face, or crawled out of his mat at the presence of this possible Man of God, he would at once have done so. But he was paralyzed. He had not even been able to hang onto the sides of his own mat as the rope cradle lowered it. All he could do was turn his head away, close his eyes and wish, or pray, to disappear.

"Son!" The voice which summoned Judah was gentle as a mother's calling a favored child, but it had within it the power that could summon worlds into being. Turning his head toward the sound of the voice, Judah opened his eyes, feeling only the desire to say with Isaiah, "Woe is me! I am doomed. For I am a man of unclean lips, living among a people of unclean lips, yet my eyes have seen the King, the Lord of hosts!" Indeed, he had opened his mouth to recite the plea, when Jesus smiled at him. "Your sins are forgiven!" He said, and Judah felt the weight of his misery, his despair, his anger, his uncleanness, so dark in the presence of this Man of God, lift from him, as clouds are lifted from the face of the blazing sun, or the weight of illness is lifted from the body as health returns. Judah returned the smile Jesus gave him and, for a moment, there was utter stillness and light between them, binding them to each other in love and a kind of silent, singing joy.

Then Judah was aware of a kind of static in the room, a crackling discontent that struck him like a blow. He saw the kindly face of Ezra, whose house roof he had just come through, looking worried, and the pinched face of Asa take on a particularly sour expression. Eli looked as if he had won a victory over a hated and feared enemy by a subtle trick, while Jonas grimaced in disgruntled surprise, as if he had bitten into a very sour grape and his own tongue at the same moment. Why were they so upset? They weren't saying anything, which was unusual for these experts on the Law and unofficial rulers of the town. They were always ready to pronounce authoritatively on anything, especially if people didn't much want them to.

Maybe it was his presence there, in front of the Holy Man! Judah could understand the reaction, for it had been his own. Further, these four had made it very clear that, in their judgement, he had been quite justly paralyzed by God as a punishment for his sins.

But then, why weren't they as happy as he was now? For the Man of God had just forgiven all his sins--so now he was cleansed and a joy to all Israel! Now he could stay in the presence of the Man of God without fear of annihilation, and they could be glad because, forgiven, he would not contaminate the air Jesus breathed and they breathed with him!

They ought, Judah reflected, to be leading dances of joy not curdling all the milk in the village! What was the matter with them? Unless, of course, they didn't believe Jesus was the Man of God. That might explain the discontent, and the fear even. For if they thought Jesus was just anybody, then His forgiving sins would be blasphemy, Jesus claiming to be God and usurping God's power.

How dreadful for them! Judah felt a stab of compassion. These poor scholars--to be so in the dark, not to know, as he did now, by his experience, that Jesus was the Man of God! "I must tell them!" he thought urgently. "Jesus can forgive sin! He just did, really did, forgive mine! My sins are gone, absolutely and completely! He is God's Man, not a blasphemer! I must make them know that, so they can be happy too!"

But as he opened his mouth to speak, Judah heard

the voice of Jesus, answering the argument they had not spoken aloud. "Why do you harbor these thoughts?" He said to them, as if He were asking them why they kept scorpions in their beds, or drank poison instead of wine. There was compassion mingled with the correction, the same concern Judah had felt in his own heart, but in its perfect form. Judah relaxed. Jesus would tell them what they needed to know. Good! It would be all right.

Having paused to allow His first question to register, Jesus asked a second, "Which is easier: to say 'Your sins are forgiven you' or to say 'Get up and walk'?"

There, thought Judah with satisifaction. They had to be able to see that! For the Man of God, to speak was to create, purity or health, it did not matter. Whatever He said would come at once into being, just because He had spoken the word summoning it. They had to be able to feel the force of that power in Him! After all, they were the learned ones, not he, and if he knew himself to be forgiven and cleansed, made whole in spirit and one with God by Jesus' word, they would have to, now that He had explained it! Judah smiled at Jesus with delight. In a minute the soured four in their misery and dark would see what Jesus had said and Judah already knew, and they would have to rejoice. They couldn't help it!

Jesus smiled back at Judah, with a love that took his breath away, but the Master's next words were addressed, not to Judah, but to the four and all those around them, a fact which disconcerted Judah not at all. He could wait, for he was safe in God's love; theirs was the more urgent need."In any case," Jesus was saying, looking at them one by one, gazing deep into their eyes and into their very souls, "to make it clear to you that the Son of Man has authority on earth to forgive sins," and he turned his gaze on Judah. He drew a deep breath and paused. His smile carried with its love both a blaze of glory and a hint of anticipatory pleasure. He had something in mind to do that Judah had not yet seen, and, it seemed to the paralyzed man,

Jesus was looking forward to revealing the surprise to him with the same impatient delight he himself had felt when he had surprised Ruth with the bolt of red silk she had longed for and never dreamed she would ever have. But Jesus had already forgiven his sins. What more could there be?

As if Judah had spoken aloud, Jesus' smile deepened, and He exhaled with a sound that was almost a laugh. "I say to you," He said directly to Judah in a ringing tone, "get up! Take your mat with you and return to your house!"

There was a concerted gasp from all of the crowd within earshot, but Judah barely heard it. He was aware only that the Master had summoned him to life by the power of His love, and that his one desire was to do exactly what Jesus had commanded, at once. Swiftly he sat up, tucked his legs under him, knelt, and stood. Stepping off the mat he rolled it quickly and tucked it under his arm. The health he felt flowing through his limbs was the physical version of the health he had felt flowing through his entire being when Jesus had forgiven his sins, and his joy at the second healing was a mirroring of his joy at the first. He stood erect before Jesus for a moment, his whole soul's love and all his joy expressed in the single look he gave Jesus. Then he bowed and turned to finish doing what Jesus had commanded; he was going home.

The crowds as they caught sight of him began to cheer. Above Judah, looking down on the scene through the hole in the roof, Jonathan laughing and crying at the same time pounded his brother Saul on the back. "We did it!" the younger man kept shouting, his voice all but drowned in the chorus of shouts coming from the crowd below.

In the street, Ruth who had managed to get close to Ezra's house, had seen Jonathan and his friends taking Judah up to the roof on his mat. She had not seen anything else, but when she heard Jesus' command her heart obeyed. She, too, rose in spirit from the paralysis in which Judah's despair, though not his injury, had been holding her captive, and as her beloved emerged from Ezra's house she began to sing softly a passage from Isaiah, both for Judah and for Jesus:

"Rise up in splendor! Your light has come,
The glory of the Lord shines upon you.
See, darkness covers the earth,
and thick clouds cover the peoples;
But upon you the Lord shines,
and over you appears His glory.
Nations shall walk by your light,
and kings by your shining radiance.
Raise your eyes and look about;
they all gather and come to you
Your sons come from afar
and your daughters in the arms of their nurses.
Then shall you be radiant at what you see;
your heart shall throb and overflow..."

While she sang, she made her way toward Judah, before whom the crowd parted. At last she faced him, the love in her shining like a flame, meeting his and merging with it.

Behind them they heard the crowd crying out praise to God and shouting its wonder and joy. "We have never seen anything like this!" they exclaimed in a hundred ways at once.

Under the jubilant racket Judah stood looking down into Ruth's radiant eyes. He took her hand. "My wife?" he said shyly. "Beloved? Will you come with me to our house?"

"I've been waiting for you to ask me," she replied simply, her smile blinding in its joy.

"Come, then," he said, smiling in his turn, and hand in hand they began to walk home together.

Moses and The Burning Bush

Sheep, the shepherd reflected, were just as stubborn as those Hebrews he had left behind, and just as unconscious of their own best interests. They smelled about the same, too, he added wryly, wrinkling his nose as a slight breeze, blowing in his direction, reminded him of this second resemblance. Still, shepherding the flocks of his Midianite father-in-law, Jethro, with a sound home, a good meal, a welcoming wife and a loving son to return to was a thousand times preferable to death at the ungentle hands of the Pharaoh's executioners. Even having to grow a beard only reduced the preference factor to 850.

The man grinned as he ran his fingers through his now respectable beard. At least it had stopped itching, and he was getting used to keeping it out of things, and things out of it. Physically he might almost pass for the Midianites among whom he was living, or for the Hebrew he was by birth, except that he hadn't been circumcised, of course. Psychically, the matter was somewhat more complicated.

Settling himself in the sparse shade of a rock outcropping, the shepherd recalled for the thousandth time what he knew of his strange history. The review would end, he knew, at the single, unanswered, perhaps unanswerable, question, which sat foursquare in the center of his consciousness and, like the store-city the Israelites had had to build for Pharaoh, blocked every path and dominated his internal horizons. Why?

Nevertheless, he began again to unravel the complicated weaving that had become himself at this moment, tracing strand by strand each element and placing each event, as though by faithful exactness and concentrated attention he might, this time, surprise the secret from its cunning net.

To begin with, he had been born at an unfortunate
period in Israel's history. It was after the Pharaoh's
decree that all male Hebrew babies were to be killed, to
keep this population of slaves from so far outnum-
bering their masters that a slave rebellion might be
feasible. Forgotten was the service of Joseph, the
Hebrew slave, to Egypt in the time of the seven years'
famine. Thanks to Joseph's God-given reading of
Pharaoh's prophetic dream, Egypt had warehoused
grain surpluses for the seven years of plenty preceding
the seven years of famine. Thus, when the rest of the
region was beginning to starve, they turned to Egypt
where, alone, they could purchase grain.

Joseph, the God-sent dream reader, who had proved
his fidelity as well as his administrative effectiveness
previously, had been put in charge of the operation. He
supervised first the filling of the granaries, and then
the distribution of the grain to the Egyptians and its
sale to foreigners. Thus, as Yahweh had saved him,
he had been able to save his own father and brothers
from starvation (though the brothers had sold him into
slavery in the first place). In reward for his service to
Egypt, Joseph had been instructed by Pharaoh to welcome his whole family, some seventy strong, to Egypt,
where they were to live as honored citizens.

The shepherd shifted his position on the ground,
swatted an exploring insect and grunted wryly. How
short was the memory of men for favors bestowed--then
as now! Resolutely he turned his mind from the present to the past, resisting the temptation to wallow in
self-pity. That was no way to find an answer to
anything.

So the Egyptians had forgotten the gift of life that had
come to them through a Hebrew's dream and Yahweh
who had sent it, and as time passed had enslaved the
alien people living in their midst. Yahweh had blessed
them, however, and by the time of the shepherd's birth,
the ruling Pharaoh, made nervous by the increased
Hebrew population, had already tried to persuade the
midwives to destroy the male children born to Hebrew

mothers and had failed. Not that the women defied him--they simply "didn't get there on time," they declared when Pharaoh, receiving the report that the numbers of male Hebrew children were not decreasing, had them questioned. It was these midwives' unaccountable "slowness" which had allowed the shepherd's older brother Aaron, the middle child of the family, to survive.

Indirect methods having failed, Pharaoh went to direct slaughter, ordering "all his subjects" to cast all male babies into the river, though the girls might be allowed to live. But when the shepherd was born, his mother had resolved to defy the decree. She kept this third child, her second son, safely hidden for the first months of its life and then, unable to conceal him any longer, she had woven a papyrus basket, waterproofed it with pitch and bitumen, and, placing the baby in it, had hidden this tiny "boat" among the reeds near the river bank.

Miriam, the eldest child, safe because she was a girl, had stationed herself nearby to keep watch over her baby brother. Because she was hardly more than a child herself, no one paid any attention to her or observed her peculiar attachment to one portion of the river bank.

And then the second major strand of the weaving of his life had been threaded in. Pharaoh's daughter, coming down the river to bathe, had discovered the tiny craft, had it fished out of the water and brought to her and opened. "A male child!" she had exclaimed. "It must be one of the Hebrew children!"

"Please, ma'am," a voice by her elbow had interrupted, and the Princess had jumped. Then looking down she had found a small girl standing beside her. Miriam had always had the gift of appearing as wise or as ingenuous as she wished, the shepherd recalled with a slight smile, and now she desired to seem far younger than her ten years. "Please, ma'am," she had said again, touching the sleeve of the Princess' tunic. "Would you like me to fetch a Hebrew woman to nurse the baby for you?"

"Thank you, little one," the Princess had replied, amazed at such good sense in what seemed to her a child of five. "Will you do that for me?"

Without a word Miriam had turned and trotted off, and, as soon as she was out of sight of the royal party, had sped to her own home. She quickly fetched her mother, bringing her to where the Princess was waiting, lovingly cuddling the infant which she had removed from its basket, cooing Egyptian endearments at which the baby was crowing with delight. "Please, ma'am," said Miriam, again becoming five to her mother's well-concealed astonishment, "Here is the woman."

"Thank you, little one," smiled the Princess, and as she turned to the mother holding out the child, Miriam silently effaced herself. "Will you nurse this child for me?" asked the Princess, who preferred to be direct when she could. "I shall pay you for your services, of course," she added, when the shepherd's mother failed to reply. The Princess, not a patient woman, though, within her limits, fairly perceptive, had assumed the woman's silence was a reluctance economically or politically motivated, and by her offer had sought to remove obstacles in both classes.

The shepherd's mother, mastering the astonishment which had silenced her at this unexpected turn of events, replied hastily. "Oh no! I mean, yes! Yes, certainly I will nurse the child, but payment... no!"

"I insist!" declared the Princess grandly. She was not a Pharaoh's daughter for nothing, and knew her orders had a better chance of being faithfully followed if a monthly cash stipend served the woman as a timely reminder of whose child this was, and why all care must be taken of him! "When he is weaned you must bring him to me," she had continued, handing the baby over, "but until then, keep him safe," and she had looked meaningfully at the woman.

The shepherd's mother, clutching the baby, had looked straight at the Princess. "I shall care for him as

I would care for my own child, my Lady!" she assured the Princess, and bowing deeply had turned and almost run toward her own house.

"Odd!" murmured the Princess watching her swiftly retreating figure. "I didn't know my father's decrees had so much force among these people that they would hesitate even to seem to disobey them. The woman is entirely safe to obey me; why does she scurry away so quickly hiding the child? A poor weak creature," concluded the royal lady shrugging. "Now I should like to have seen that baby's mother! There must be a woman of force indeed!" And the Princess had gone to the river to do the bathing her discovery of the infant had interrupted. "When the nurse brings the child back," she reflected, slipping into the coolness of the reed-shadowed river, "I shall adopt him and name him Moses, for I drew him out of the water."

The Princess fulfilled her resolve. When the shepherd's mother had brought the three-year old to the Pharaoh's daughter's apartment, the Princess had received the child with delight, and "Moses," for so he was to be known, was at once made a member of her household.

The shepherd remembered the mothering the Egyptian princess had given him far more clearly than he did the care of his own mother, or that of the faithful Miriam and her patient shadow Aaron. The Pharaoh's daughter had seen to it that her "son" received every advantage in upbringing and education the royal household could offer. Politics, royal intrigues, economics, religion, history, the management of men--all entered into the liberal education the Princess planned and provided.

She also saw to it that he knew he was not an Egyptian by birth but by her gift and choice. He was taught his true connection to the despised race of Hebrew slaves and was told of his dramatic rescue from certain death by the Princess herself. The royal "mother" intended to bind her handsome, foundling son to her even more securely than his own natural instincts had already done, and indeed, the shepherd acknowledged, he had been, and still was, grateful to her for her timely rescue and for the pains she had taken to bring him to accomplished manhood.

But the news of his Hebrew origins had wakened in him, not repulsion, but a curiosity about his own people and their history, and he had spent much time piecing together a coherent account of their origins and adventures before their coming to Egypt and their subsequent enslavement. In fact, he had even learned enough Hebrew to speak to his people in their own language, a feat he did not announce at court, where he was seen as a promising Egyptian courtier, the princess' protege, and nothing more.

It was several years now since the climactic event occurred which had led him to his present place as a member of Jethro's household. Remembering, Moses winced.

The day had been hot. He had been unusually restless and so had gone walking again down by the construction sites, a habit which had been growing on him since the decree imposing even harsher forced labor upon "his people," the Hebrews, had been promulgated. He could not help these suffering workers, and to his own disgust hardly dared acknowledge even to himself his blood kinship with them, lest he be plucked from the luxury he enjoyed behind the Princess' protective, if unofficial, authority and thrust into the mud where these people sweated, struggled and died. He was afraid to be a Hebrew but unwilling to forget that he was one, and so he writhed in the twin fires of fear and remorse, and took long walks through the construction areas, apparently a haughty Egyptian of the Princess' household out to observe the curiosities of slave-existence.

On this day, however, the aristocratic "Egyptian" had stepped out of character. He had seen the master of a small gang of slaves pull one of them, a young man, out of the ranks. He sent the others on their way with his assistant, and when the two were alone, with a slow smile of growing satisfaction, he methodically whipped the slave until the youth was near death. It was the gloating smile of the Egyptian that had broken Moses' years of prudent concealment and helpless, contemptuous, rage. Quickly he had glanced about. There was no one in sight but the slave and his tormentor. Moses had stepped forward, killed the Egyptian with a single, deadly blow as he had been taught by his military instructor, buried the body in the sand and disappeared.

The act had pleased him. It was, however hidden, a concrete declaration of his true allegiance to the Hebrew people, his people. But the act worried him as well. Suppose someone had seen him? But no one could have seen him, he assured himself, as, the next afternoon, he went walking again. Approaching the area where he had seen the atrocity which galvanized him into unaccustomed action, Moses turned sharply. At the end of the street he could see two men, slaves and Hebrews by their dress, in violent argument. As he drew near enough to hear the quarrel, Moses saw one of the men strike the other a vicious blow. In two strides Moses had caught the offender's hand upraised for another blow. "Why do you strike your fellow Hebrew?" he asked.

But the man, though he squirmed in Moses' powerful grip did not cringe at the sight of the man in the clothing of the Egyptian royal household. Instead, he sneered, "Who has appointed you ruler and judge over us?" adding through clenched teeth as Moses spun him around locking his arm behind his back, "Are you thinking of killing me as you did the Egyptian?"

For a split second, blood pounding in his ears, the enraged Moss was about to do precisely that. How dare this insolent slave...! And then, like a pot of cold water dumped on his head, came the realization, "What I have done is known." With an extra twist of the arm he held, Moses flung the man from him and turned on his heel, sweat beginning to run down his back. If his deed was known, his life was not safe here, but where could he go? But was it known?

The question was answered for him that evening as he passed a buzzing knot of his associates huddled in front of the entrance to the Princess' palace after dinner. As he passed them he overhead broken phrases, "Slave master," "One blow," "in the sand like a common slave," "slave dying nearby said it was an Egyptian," "our household," "death penalty," "Pharaoh's wrath."   Not breaking stride he went to his quarters, gathered his most precious possessions and slipped out into the night.

He had never been able to say exactly how he had found Midian nor to decide why he had happened to choose to rest at the well Jethro's daughters used to water their father's flocks, nor to understand why, of all days, this should be the one that shepherds should chase the priest's daughters and their flocks from the trough they had filled so that their own beasts might drink. But so it had happned, and Moses, hopeless on his own account, had struck out at these bullies with all the rage that he had no way to use in his own defense. If he died for this third uncharacteristic interference, he had reflected, he would at least have done something to redeem his forty years of complacent passivity as a fradulent "Egyptian."

But he did not die. The girls, sent back to the well by their father after Jethro had been told the tale of their rescue, had found him sitting there, in a lethargy born as much of despairing bewilderment about what to do in his exile as of physical exertion. They brought him home with them as Jethro had commanded, and gave him a meal. Jethro, a priest of the Midianite people, had welcomed this stranger, offered him a home with them, given him his daughter Zipporah in marriage, and the union had been blessed with a son, Gershom.

Now that he had lived in Jethro's household for several years, Moses understood better his father-in-law's motivations and the rather limited actual risk the priest had taken. At the time the fleeing Israelite had been overwhelmed by the "no questions asked" attitude of Jethro and by his unquestioning welcome of an alien into his home as a guest, and into his household as a permanent member.

Effectively, he had ceased to exist as far as the rest of the world was concerned, once he had stepped into Jethro's tent, eaten his bread and accepted Jethro's daughter as his wife. He was safe from Egyptian pursuit, for the bearded Midianites, though not Hebrews, were descendants of Abraham, and would protect even a distant kinsman against foreign attack.

But he was not, on that account, a free agent. He was as bound to Jethro and his clan as he had ever been to the Egyptians through Pharaoh's daughter's adoption of him, and if he failed here, there would be no escape by flight.

He was fully aware that, if he so much as speculated upon behavior which would defile the guest-friend/host bond or defy the Midianite marriage conventions, he would simply vanish in this herders' wilderness without a trace; should anyone happen to miss him and make inquiries, there would be no answer.

And so here he was, minding a recalcitrant flock of sheep--a Hebrew by birth who was permanently separated from his family, if any were alive; an Egyptian by culture, education, upbringing and, he admitted, by preference, who could not set foot inside the boundaries of the country, much less inside the palace where he felt most at home in this world and had been most welcomed and loved; and an adopted Midianite, tied by affection to his wife, their child and her family, and bound by gratitude and loyalty, as well as by a lively sense of self-preservation, to sustain at any cost the clan and its enterprises for the rest of his life. Why?

The review had ended, as the shepherd knew it must, with the unaswerable question still unanswered and still demanding a response. Why should he not simply be grateful to God and Jethro that he had escaped Pharaoh's vengeance, and be content with loving the wife who cherished him, nurturing the child who was the delight of his life, and doing the useful work that lay to hand? It was a good life! Why could he not be happy in it? Why did he have to keep beating his head against the unanswerable "Why?" "Enough!" he said aloud, and rising began to call the sheep. He wanted them further up the mountain before sunset, near the stream in that meadow he could just see.

For once the beasts were almost cooperative, and as afternoon shadows began to lengthen Moses settled them in what would be their pasture for some time to come. He was pleased. The desert crossing had not been all that difficult and now that they had gotten to Horeb they could all stay put for a while.

His eyes, traveling idly over the pasture he had selected, noting again the stream, the sheltering rocks and the bushes that appeared intermittently in the grassland, Moses suddenly froze. What was that to the left? It looked like a bush that had just burst into orange flame, but that was impossible, thought Moses as he moved toward the bush. It must be an effect of sunlight on the blossoms, for if it were fire the bush would have disappeared by now, and he could still see green leaves. Besides, a fire that size would sweep...He stifled the thought without completing it, and doubled his pace.

Within five feet of the bush, as Moses saw that, beyond a doubt, this was flame engulfing the still green-leaved bush, not blossoms and not sunlight, he heard a Voice that stopped him in mid-stride.

"Moses! Moses!" said the Voice. It seemed to come from the burning bush, or from that direction. Though the Voice's power had an elemental force that Moses somehow knew to be capable of summoning worlds into existence, or of annihilating them at will, it did not evoke fear.

Hearing the Voice speak his own name, Moses felt only the sense of being, at last, completed, and experienced an upsurge of love that took his breath away. "Here I am!" he said when he could talk again, and his voice was closer to song than to speech.

"Come no nearer," instructed the Voice, and Moses drew back his leading foot to place it quietly beside the other. "Remove your sandals," the Voice continued, explaining in an almost conversational tone, as Moses bent to obey, "The ground you are standing on is holy."

When Moses was again standing, his feet bare and his sandals behind him, the Voice went on, resuming the world-summoning tone that was apparently its proper one, and once again Moses felt his overwhelming surge of love in response to the sense of being, word by word, moment by moment, breath by breath, simultaneously expanded, deepened and newly completed by the Voice's speaking.

"I am the God of your fathers," the Voice declared, "the God of Abraham, the God of Isaac and God of Jacob."

At that enunciation of what his body and psyche already knew, Moses' mind was hushed, the internal monologue entirely stilled in an awe that sent him in a crouch to one knee as his left arm rose to shield his eyes and cover his head from the blow that must, surely, descend, for even Egyptians knew that no mortal might see God and live. But even as he waited he knew no fear, only expectation and a joy deeper than any he had ever known.

The Voice went on, apparently taking no notice of the auditor's response. "I have seen the miserable state of My people in Egypt. I have heard their appeal to be free of their slave-drivers. Yes, I am well aware of their sufferings." Listening, Moses wondered if the Voice, the Lord God, rather, also knew of the reaction of his people when someone tried to give them a hand by removing one of those slave-drivers, but the Voice swept on giving him no time to raise the issue.

"I mean," said the Lord God, "to deliver them out of the hands of the Egyptians and bring them up out of that land to a land where milk and honey flow, the home of the Canaanites, the Hittites, the Amorites, the Perizzites, the Hivites and the Jebusites. And now the cry of the sons of Israel has come to me, and I have witnessed the way in which the Egyptians oppress them, so come! I send you to Pharaoh, to bring the sons of Israel, My people, out of Egypt."

At that Moses lowered his left arm as he felt his jaw drop in astonishment. He could not have heard what his ears assured him had just been said. He stared at the bush where the leaping flames continued to lick at the green leaves without, he noted absently, even scorching their edges. He knew from his Egyptian training, as well as from his Hebrew and creaturely instincts, that it was not polite, and certainly not prudent, to stare at a human superior; what rudeness and folly then, to stare at the Voice, at the Lord God rather-- no, at the place from which the Lord God had chosen to speak!

But he could not help himself. This was too much! He, an exile with a death warrant out for him, was to go to Pharaoh and demand the release of an economically essential slave population from this supreme ruler in Egypt who was assumed to be, and was worshipped as, the manifestation of Ra, the sun god? Even as it protested the incongruity and impossibility of what the Voice had asked, one part of Moses' mind hooted irreverently. Sun god! If the Pharaoh were ever to hear this Voice, he might re-think his claims to divinity and rule Egypt from a more modest throne!

But still, how could he go? Then again, how could he refuse? Moses became aware that, in the stretching silence, the Voice, rather, the Lord God, was waiting and had been waiting for some time. He gulped. He had to say something! "Who," he croaked. He cleared his throat and tried again. "Who am I to go to Pharaoh and bring the sons of Israel out of Egypt?" It was by no means a full statement of the dilemma, but it was a start, and Moses had learned in Pharaoh's court that, if one had to speak an objection, it was better to begin with a minimal statement and expand it, than to say everything at once and find oneself headed for summary execution.

The Voice answered the objection as if a modest self-judgement had been the only source of the speaker's objection. "I shall be with you," said the Lord in an encouraging tone, adding, "and this is the sign by which you shall know that it is I who have sent you. After you have led the people out of Egypt, you are to offer worship to God on this very mountain."

So much for modesty, thought the shepherd. He tugged at his beard and temporized, "I am to go, then, to the sons of Israel and say to them, 'The God of your fathers has sent me to you?' But if they ask me what his name is, what am I to tell them?" As he asked this daring question, Moses held his breath. To know a man's true name was to have power over him. Would the God of Israel, his God as a son of Israel, he remembered with a slight jump, answer him, a refugee in flight both from the enslaved Hebrew people and from the Egyptians who had adopted and then proscribed him?

Apparently he would. In a tone of increased force and increased love that fell on Moses, syllable by syllable, with the weight of the separate stone blocks used in the construction of the pyramids, the Voice declared, "I Am Who Am." After a pause in which Moses began to breathe again, the Lord added slowly, "This is what you must say to the sons of Israel: 'I AM has sent me to you.'" The Voice repeated, still more slowly, "You are to say to the sons of Israel: 'Yahweh, the God of your fathers, the God of Abraham, the God of Isaac and the God of Jacob, has sent me to you.'" Then the Voice added quietly, each word a separate sun illuminating the listening shepherd's inner horizons, "This is My Name for all time; by this Name I shall be invoked for all generations to come."

The fire still burned in the bush, which was still unconsumed by it. His eyes told him that, but Moses felt as though the fire, bush and all, had been transferred from the pasture to the center of his soul. All prudence, all fear, all hesitation vanished in that fire, and the one desire of his heart was to pour itself out in a single shout of, "Yes! I'll go! Yes, Lord! Whatever you say!" That desire, rising in his throat, met the downward force of his Egyptian-trained mind, now recovered from its momentary paralysis, which was shouting with equal conviction, "No! I can't go! I can't do it! It's impossible!"

The collision of these contrary forces met at Moses' quivering tongue and silenced him as effectively as a blow to the windpipe. He said nothing, and the Voice went on, either not seeing, or choosing to ingore, the struggle taking place in the trembling man. "Go and gather the elders of Israel together," instructed the Lord God, "and tell them, 'Yahweh, the God of your fathers has appeared to me--the God of Abraham, of Issac and of Jacob, and He has said to me, I HAVE VISITED YOU AND SEEN ALL THAT THE EGYPTIANS ARE DOING TO YOU. AND SO I HAVE RESOLVED TO BRING YOU UP OUT OF EGYPT WHERE YOU ARE OPPRESSED, INTO THE LAND OF THE CANAANITES, THE HITTITES, THE AMORITES, THE PERIZZITES, THE HIVITES, AND THE JEBUSITES TO A LAND WHERE MILK AND HONEY FLOW. They will listen to your words," the Voice went on as Moses, opening his mouth to object, closed it again, "and with the elders of Israel you are to go to the King of Egypt and say to him, 'Yahweh the God of the Hebrews has come to meet us. Give us leave, then, to make a three-days' journey into the wilderness to offer sacrifice to Yahweh, our God.'"

The Voice paused, but Moses said nothing. His silence was the silence of the mallet-stunned ox just before the descent of the knife that would take its life in sacrifice, but the Lord God apparently took it for a silence of comprehending agreement. At any rate, in a tone of grim satisfaction that made the hair on the back of Moses' neck rise, the Voice continued, "For Myself, knowing that the king of Egypt will not let you go unless he is forced by a mighty hand, I shall show my power and strike Egypt with all the wonders I am going to work there. After that, he will let you go." Then, as Moses continued silent, the Lord said encouragingly, "I will give the people such prestige in the eyes of the Egyptians that, when you go, you will not go empty-handed. Every woman will ask her neighbor and the woman who is staying in her house for silver ornaments and gold. With these you will adorn your sons and daughters. You will plunder the Egyptians!" The voice ended, and the triumphant joy in the tone roused Moses from his stunned silence at last.

He took a deep breath and sighed, shaking his head. It was such a lovely dream. It was a shame that it could never happen. But it couldn't. Now, though, he had to tell God that His plan wouldn't work. Better begin with the Hebrews and their recalcitrance. Gently he asked, "What if they will not believe me, or listen to my words, and say to me, 'Yahweh has not appeared to you?'" It was a probable Hebrew response, Moses knew, and it was insurmountable. He waited.

"What is that in your hand?" asked the Voice with a suspicious smoothness.

Warily Moses replied, "A staff." Swiftly, his gaze travelled up and down its six-foot length, and then he looked back at the bush.

The fire seemed to flare higher. "Throw it on the ground," came the command, the tone still smooth as the flow of oil. Moses obeyed. As the staff touched the ground between the shepherd and the bush it became a serpent, which at once turned its head and darting tongue away from the flaming bush and began to move in a swift, ground-devouring slither toward Moses.

The shepherd had jumped to his feet and sprung back instantly, but before he could turn to run the Voice spoke again. "Put out your hand," came the command, "and catch it by the tail!" Moses obeyed at once, with a speed and completeness his Egyptian military training had made a reflex. As his right hand shot out and grasped the cool, scaly, living tail of the serpent, he felt the tail change to bark on wood. He looked down. There was his shepherd's staff, all six feet of it, as if it had never been anything else.

Moses shuddered, and came back to his present circumstances with the realization that the Voice had been speaking and that the tone, though essentially

serious, was faintly amused. Blushing, he picked up
the words in mid-sentence,"... so that they may believe
that Yahweh, the God of their fathers, the God of
Abraham, the God of Isaac, and the God of Jacob, has
really appeared to you."

There was a significant pause. Moses, with five
wildly disordered sentences struggling for utterance,
said nothing, and looked back down at his staff. He
shuddered again. That had been too real a demonstration! But... The Voice interrupted. "Put your hand
in your bosom!" Moses looked at the bush for a moment. Then he watched his left hand rise and slip
obediently into his tunic next to his skin. He could feel
it there, cold and trembling slightly as it lay over his
diaphragm. He waited a moment, and then, with an
inquiring look toward the bush, drew the hand out
again.

He looked down at it and gasped. He had leprosy!
The hand had turned white, had covered with
swellings and open, infected, sores, had twisted in on
itself and had shrunk forming the claw that he had
seen so often on beggars, seen and shrunk from. His
gasp was harsh, and sweat standing on his forehead
and back ran down in rivulets.

"Put your hand back in your bosom," came the
command, and repressing a shudder Moses did as he
was told. He did not want to take it out again, ever, but
almost against his will, he drew it out, as his eyes
sought and found the burning bush. Then dragging his
gaze from the bright flames he looked down. The hand
was as it had been. He shook it a little and turned it
over and then back. No leprosy there! Not a trace!

Moses exhaled, shaking his head, but did not get a
chance to formulate what troubled him about the
demonstrations, for the Voice was speaking again,
persuasively, almost, Moses thought, as if the Lord God
felt the need to convince him when he could simply
command, and annihilate him if he refused to obey! It
was all so unthinkable! The shepherd shook his head
again and concentrated on what the Voice was saying.

"Even so," came the words, "should they not believe you nor be convinced by the first sign, the second will convince them. But if they should believe neither of these two signs and not listen to your words, you must take water from the river and pour it on the ground, and the water you have drawn from the river will turn to blood on the ground."

Again there was a silence. The Lord God was waiting for Moses to agree to do His bidding, and the shepherd, his love at war with his fear, his trust outshouted by his Hebrew common sense and Egyptian prudence, could only shake his head helplessly.

It was his experience at the Egyptian court, observing the variously skilled ambassadors in their dealings with the Pharaoh that suggested a way out of his dilemma. "But my Lord," he began. His tone was so oily in its placation that he winced and altered it. "Never in my life," he began again, "have I been a man of eloquence, either before or after You spoke to me, your servant. I am a slow speaker, and not able to speak well!"

There was a silence in which Moses heard his own words again and realized that the very cleverness of the argument--that slow speech was an insuperable obstacle to a diplomat--was proof that the claim was false. He cringed. Surely the Lord God would punish his impudence!

But the Voice replied quietly, judiciously considering and dealing with the objection as though it had not destroyed itself. "Who gave a man his mouth?" asked the Lord. "Who makes him dumb or deaf, gives him sight or leaves him blind? Is it not I, Yahweh?" And then, with a hint of impatience, the Voice concluded, "Now go! And I shall help you to speak and tell you what to say."

"Please Lord!" wailed Moses, deserted alike by his Egyptian cunning and Hebrew courage, "Please! Send anyone You like." He extended his hands as he fell to his knees and his staff fell to the ground, rolled and lay still. He did not add, "Don't send me!" He didn't have to. The message was as plain as the plea was, in Moses' judgement, cowardly, but he could no more have refrained from making the plea than he could have held back the tears that rose in his eyes and made his voice quiver.

He waited. There was a pause, and then the flames surrounding the bush suddenly shot higher, as if the Lord had had enough. When the Voice sounded it cut the air like the whiplash of the Egyptian slave-driver Moses had killed, and Moses shrank back. "There is your brother Aaron, the Levite, is there not?" demanded the Lord. "I know that he is a good speaker!"

Moses nodded, too frightened to speak, and the Voice grew calmer, though no less commanding. "Here he comes to meet you. When he sees you, his heart will be full of joy. You will speak to him, and tell him what message to give." As Moses nodded again and opened his mouth to speak, the Voice went on more re-assuringly, "I shall help you to speak, and him too, and instruct you what to do. He himself is to speak to the people in your place." Then with the same undertone of faint amusement that had attended the return of the serpent to the staff form, the Lord added, "He will be your mouthpiece and you will be the god inspiring him!"

Thinking of the Egyptian priests and magicians and their habitual behavior in presenting dubious oracles through fradulent mediums, Moses smiled and his eyes flashed. This would show them all up--especially when Yahweh worked His wonders on behalf of His people. This was scary, but it would be fun! He could do it! Moses had turned from the bush to see if he could find the figure of the approaching Aaron on the horizon when the Voice spoke again. The amusement was still there, but it was modulated into the tender, summoning love that had struck Moses to the heart when the Lord had first called him by name. "And take this staff into your hand!" the Voice reminded him gently. Moses, flashing a grin at the bush, reached at once for his staff, as the Lord continued, "With it you will perform the signs."

As Moses opened his mouth to whisper "Yes, Lord I will," the flames around the bush flared up once and then vanished. The bush stood there, undeniably and entirely intact, its green leaves still trembling slightly from the rush of the flame but not even faintly scorched. Moses stared at it for a moment, caught in love and wonder. Then murmuring, "Yahweh! Yahweh!" he turned, staff in hand, to find Aaron running toward him with arms outspread and a joyous smile on his face. "Brother!" he cried out, and, moving toward him, Moses replied, "Brother! Our God has spoken to me and to you this day! Listen, now, just listen!"

The Canaanite Woman's Daughter

Doris was angry, more angry than her husband Dagon could remember seeing her. "I won't have it, do you hear?" she hissed, her hands clenched. "I will not have it!"

"But what can you do? What can I do? What can anyone do? That's how she is, and there's no way to fix it. What choice do we have?"

"I tell you, as I live and breathe," his wife repeated even more vehemently, "I will not have it! Not for you, not for myself, not for this unethical ass of a doctor, not for anyone on earth! I will not have it!"

"Not even for Phyllis?" asked Dagon softly. Phyllis was their only child, a girl of eight, and the heart of her mother's heart.

"Especially not for Phyllis! How can you use her name to ask me--that! You are getting to be as un-scrupulous, as feral, as greedy, as selfish as that beast masked in his Hippocratic pieties you call a doctor. He's no doctor! He's the snake that winds around his own staff--and I hope he bites himself where it'll really do him damage!"

Dagon sighed. This was getting them nowhere, and it certainly wasn't helping their daughter. Phyllis had been suffering seizures of increasing severity over the last two years, and the doctor, a humane man for all Doris' furious accusations, had tried all the usual remedies without success. The seizures were begin-ning to threaten the child's life, as she clawed at her face and threw herself onto the ground, grinding her teeth, biting her tongue, banging her head and limbs into any object in her way. Her strength was greater than that of three healthy adults when she was in the grip of her "disease," for so they had all called it out loud, though

Dagon was fairly certain he was not the only one to suspect the presence of an evil spirit or spirits.

At such times they could not keep her from harming herself, and she was beginning to harm those who tried to prevent her self-destructive if unconscious, flailings. Doris was still wearing the black eye Phyllis had given her with a random blow, Dagon's arms were clawed as though a wild cat had attacked him, and the physician, Alexander, was thoroughly bruised.

It was Alexander's latest suggestion that had enraged Doris. In his heart, Dagon could understand why, partly, but his reasoning mind, putting his emotions in their proper, subordinate place, agreed with the physician. Alexander had argued that since Phyllis, always something of a danger to herself, was now, with her increase of age and physical strength, becoming a danger to her family and physician as well, and since her condition was rapidly becoming worse, with more violent seizures occurring at shorter intervals and lasting for longer periods of time, she ought to be prevented from suffering any more herself and from causing any further suffering to those who cared for her.

He, Alexander, would undertake to prepare a medication which would have the desired effect. The child would drink it, would go peacefully to sleep and simply would not awaken. It would be the simplest solution, best for all of them. In any case, there was nothing more medical science could do for her. Why should her agony and her family's pain be uselessly prolonged? Since she must die shortly in any event, why should not Alexander ensure that the passage should be an easy one, rather than an agonized warfare of pain and terror, which it must inevitably be if nature were allowed to take its course?

The arguments, smooth in Alexander's presentation, accorded with Dagon's reasoning; though his feelings rebelled, he was accustomed to rule them by reason and to make his decisions without giving his emotions the power of changing his mind.

So he had concurred with Alexander's argument, accepted his judgement and tentatively agreed to his proposal. Then he presented the matter to Doris, and met an opposition as bitter and complete as it was unexpected and forceful.

"I will not have it, Dagon, and that is final," declared Doris again after a brief pause. Dagon sighed. He knew from experience that for Doris, "final" really was final, and that all the gods of the universe, rising in concert to oppose her, might just as well save their breath to cool their soup.

"Very well," he said quietly. "I'll tell Alexander we have decided to let Phyllis finish her life as the gods dictate. I hope she doesn't have to suffer too much in the process."

There was a silence. Then, with a suggestion of tears in her voice, Doris spoke. "You said 'we'. That was good of you, Dagon, really good."

"Sorry?" Dagon, for the moment, was at sea. "We?" he repeated.

"You said you'd tell Alexander we had decided," his wife explained. "That was really good of you; I know you don't agree with me in this, and that you really feel I'm wrong. Yet you said we. Thank you for that."

"Think, not feel, so it's not that good of me," replied Dagon. Then, seeing Doris's blank look he continued, "I think you're--not wrong, my dear, mistaken; I think Alexander is--has made a clearer assessment of the situation and has drawn a, well, a more expeditious conclusion. But I don't feel any of those things. My heart, in this awful time, is where it always is, right there next to yours and beating in time with it. My heart was saying the same things to me that you were-- only more vividly. So we did decide. That's the plain truth."

Silently Doris reached for her husband's hand. He took hers at once and pulled her gently into his embrace. Then she began to cry in earnest, her head tucked into his shoulder, and he held her silently, murmuring the non-words he had always used with

Phyllis when she was small, needing comfort and still able to receive and respond to it.

When her tears were finished, Doris straightened up, wiped her eyes, blew her nose and said, "I've fixed lamb for supper. Come--we'd better eat."

Dagon smiled. Doris could be counted upon never to forget to cook a meal, no matter what catastrophe was underway. She seemed to draw comfort from the process of preparing food, from a quick hearthcake to a festival banquet, and she delighted even more in watching people she loved eat and enjoy what she prepared.

That was one of the most difficult aspects of Phyllis' condition. The child was no longer interested in eating, nor could she reliably retain what she did eat. She had even stopped playing her favorite game at the table, getting food without her mother's knowledge to the entirely cooperative dogs, Spot and Brownie, who preferred to spend the dinner hour at her feet, one on either side.

Doris did not approve of having animals fed from the table, and had campaigned to have the animals barred from the kitchen altogether, but there she had not succeeded. Dagon, who had always fed his own dog from his plate, in spite of his mother's disapproval, had decreed that the dogs should stay. "The family dogs have the right to eat the family's scraps," he had declared firmly, and from that point on Spot and Brownie scavanged freely under the table, and Phyllis managed at every meal to drop them a treat or two "accidentally." As Doris always pursed her lips and frowned when Phyllis' donations became too obvious, the child quickly learned a subtletly of delivery that, her observant father reflected, would not have disgraced a professional sleight-of-hand artist!

But now Phyllis seldom came to the table for a whole meal, and, when she did, seemed not to notice Spot and Brownie, even when Doris, trying to rouse her to eat , told her she should give some of her bread or meat to "her friends" when she had eaten some herself.

That evening Phyllis had managed three spoons of soup before exhaustion overtook her. Dagon carried her to bed and Doris settled her for the night with the help of Miriam, the sixteen-year-old daughter of Agnes, Doris's sister, and her Jewish husband Ephraim. Miriam, who had been a favorite of her aunt and uncle even as a child, had become Phyllis' companion and unofficial nurse, when the seizures became serious enough to require constant attendance for Phyllis. That was before Dagon had broached Alexander's proposal.

Now, their meal finished and the dishes cleared away, and Miriam settled beside Phyllis' bed, Dagon and Doris sat together in a companionable silence which eased their pain and anxiety for their child. Drawing a deep breath, Doris straightened herself and folded her hands in her lap. Dagon looked at her alertly. This set of gestures usually meant that Doris had something to say that she considered very important. Dagon wondered what was coming.

"Dagon?"

"Yes, my love?"

"Dagon," said Doris slowly, "I've been thinking." She paused. Dagon waited. There was no point, he had long ago learned, in trying either to anticipate or to hurry Doris. She would say what she had in mind to say, in her own way and at her own pace, and that was all there was to it.

"Dagon," she said again, and again paused. Then, with a rush, "Dagon, you know in one thing you and Alexander were right. Something has to be done for Phyllis, and soon. Not what he suggested, but something."

In the silence that followed, Dagon watched Doris struggling with the problem none of them had yet been able to solve. When, at last, she looked at him, he nodded quietly. "Yes," he said simply, and that was all.

Whatever idea Doris had, and he knew from the way she sat and spoke that she had one, it was, apparently, not fully clear to her yet, and, as it was entirely hidden from him, he decided not to interfere by making random suggestions. He held himself in stillness and sat attentive and unmoving, as she worked her way through whatever labyrinth she was threading, to speak.

When finally Doris spoke it was with a hesitation rare for her. "Miriam thinks," she began slowly, "that maybe what's wrong with Phyllis isn't just a disease, the way Alexander says." She looked at him swiftly, and he was careful to keep his face noncommital, interested, and encouraging. He nodded and kept still. She continued even more slowly, her eyes fixed on him. "Miriam told me she thinks that, maybe, a devil has gotten into Phyllis."

"That has occurred to me," said Dagon slowly.

Doris was startled. "Then you don't think we're just foolish women? You think a demon could have possession of her? You think that's posible?"

As Dagon nodded, something in the way Doris was questioning him caught his attention. He couldn't quite pin it down, but one part of his mind came to focus on her manner, gestures and tone even as, with the rest of his mind he attended to her words and responded to them. "I think it's possible," he agreed. "I'm willing to say I think it's somewhere near probable, given the total failure of all Alex's remedies--and Doris, he does know his medicine."

"I know that!" His wife shook off the entire question of Alexander impatiently. "He's an excellent mechanic of the human body, none better. But, that's all he is, even if he is your friend, and while that may be enough in ordinary cases, Phyllis is not in ordinary trouble."

"Agreed," said Dagon. He had no interest in sidetracking Doris from her idea by reviving their quarrel over Alexander.

After a pause, Doris went on. "Well, anyway, Miriam says if it is a demon in Phyllis, as she thinks it could be, then the demon has to be driven out before Phyllis can get well." She stopped.

It was not clear whether she intended to continue, but Dagon, as much in the dark as he had been bfore she had spoken, hoped very much that she would. Not moving or speaking, he waited.

Finally, dropping her eyes, Doris continued, as softly as if she did not want even herself to hear what she was about to say. Dagon had to lean forward to catch the words. "Miriam says there's a man who can drive demons out of people," she reported, looking at the floor in embarrassment at having repeated this ludicrous superstition, for so she knew Dagon would view it.

When he did not laugh she ventured to look at him. "Do you think," she began, and then, with a gesture half-way between futility and rejection, looked back down at the floor. "I don't guess there could be," she finished.

To her surprise Dagon remained silent. Then he said, "Doris?"

She looked up at him. "What?" she asked.

"I've heard of men who have power over spirits," said Dagon quietly, "so if this is a demon, then a man with such power would be the one to deal with it. You said Miriam knows of one?"

"Yes," said his wife, so eagerly that Dagon was again reminded that, in spite of their harmony and the ten years of their marriage, there were areas of her inner world he did not know at all.

"Who is he?" asked Dagon. "And how can we get to him?"

"His name," reported his wife, "is Jesus. He comes from Nazareth, Miriam says, and He performs many wonders. He's made blind people see, crippled people walk; He's cleansed lepers and He's driven demons out of people. He is very kind to poor people and people in real need, but He has no patience with the people in power who try to keep Him from helping people."

"So He is a healer by trade, then?" asked Dagon.

"No, I don't think so," answered Doris slowly. "Miriam says He's primarily a teacher of a new way to live; He seems to heal people and work wonders to give people reasons to believe that what He says is true."

"So the healings are signs?"

"I guess so, though I'm not sure signs of what. Miriam has never seen Him. She's only heard about Him from her father's cousins in the Decapolis--you know, Ephraim's kin."

"He's a Jew then, this--teaching healer?" In spite of his best intentions, Dagon felt his lip curl and heard the faint contempt in his voice. He did not have much use for Jews, considering them obsessed and therefore unreliable. Some seemed to him to have focused all their energies on the exact keeping of minutiae of their Law which never let them see, not just the forest, but even a single tree, because the gnat on the bark loomed so large. The others, who had turned away from this exact observance, seemed to Dagon to be equally obsessed with the acquisition of money and increase of material possessions. In either case, the power of the obsession seemed to be so strong that, for the Jew, nothing outside of it really existed, and nothing else, certainly, had to be taken into account. Dagon trusted the judgement and actions of none of them, either inside or outside of his specialty, for Dagon believed the obsession distorted their perceptions in both spheres radically.

Doris was familiar with her husband's views of Jews and she had heard the edge in Dagon's voice, but she chose to act as though she had not. She said, "Yes, Jesus is a Jew. There's apparently serious division in the Jewish community over him, though. Miriam says the Pharisees, the fanatics about keeping their Law, simply go up in smoke whenever they argue with Him. He just takes their arguments apart the way you'd fillet a pigeon, and serves them to them on a golden platter. And the money-people can't stand the way He keeps saying that money isn't everything and that God's will should come first."

Doris paused. Dagon, looking somewhat surprised, was smiling slightly. "Enemies in both camps! That takes nerve! If those groups ever get together, He's dead. But He sounds like a most unusual Jew. Is there anyone who's for Him? I mean, besides the people He heals?"

"No organized groups, I don't think. Mostly it seems to be the poor people, farmers, fishermen, and craftsmen, and they can only go to Him when He's in their neighborhood. They can't afford to follow Him from place to place. There seems to be a small group of regulars, and an even smaller group, a dozen or so, who go with Him everywhere. But that's all, Miriam says."

"No power base, then," observed her husband. Then, as an afterthought, he remarked, "Ephraim's kin seem to be remarkably prolific correspondents!"

Doris grew slightly pink. Dagon looked at her, startled, and as he looked her face grew scarlet. She met his eyes, however, and said, "When Miriam first mentioned hearing about Jesus from Aunt Judith, I asked her to find out all she could. So she asked Aunt Judith and Aunt Judith activated the family grapevine."

"If the Emperor ever hears about your in-laws information-gathering service," Dagon remarked drily, "he'll be jealous! I don't think his people are that effective!" He smiled at Doris. "You've been thinking about taking Phyllis to see Jesus for a long time now, haven't you?" he stated, rather than asked. "Why didn't you say so?"

"I thought you'd laugh," his wife told him. "You're so quick to ridicule people's beliefs and superstitions. And I wanted to be sure for myself that this was real, because hoping and having the hope smashed is harder than never hoping at all."

"And now you're sure?" asked Dagon gently.

"Yes," she said, an edge of defiance still in her voice, even as it stiffened her shoulders and turned her slightly away from him.

"Very well," he responded. "Then we must take Phyllis to Jesus as soon as it can be managed. Did the network say when he'll be coming near here?"

"He's here now!" said Doris quickly.

"Here? Where?" asked Dagon in some surprise.

"In town. He's staying at Joab's house and Miriam found out from Esther, who's one of Ephraim's sister-in-law's cousin's--"

"Spare me!" interjected her husband.

"Well, anyway, Esther says that He really doesn't want it to get around that He is in the neighborhood. She says she thinks He's afraid if it does, all Tyre and Sidon will camp out on the doorstep for the miracles, if He does any, and nobody will listen to what He has to say. That's what Miriam says Esther says, anyway."

"I'd bet it has more to do with not rousing the Law-worshippers and the money-adorers to take united action against Him before He's ready to deal with them," offered Dagon. Then at Doris' look of surprise he said, "Look, if He actually can do all the things the network is reporting He can, it's obvious He can neutralize His enemies if He wants to. If He doesn't, it's because He's not ready to, or has something else in mind. But in any case, if we know where He is..."

"We do. Joab's house in town--and Joab is Miriam's kin."

"Then let's go there as soon as we can. Do we know how long He'll stay?"

"No," said Doris. "He never says--just goes and comes as He chooses."

"Then," said Dagon decisively, "we must make haste. We must wrap Phyllis well, put her in a litter and take her by donkey to Joab's house. We'll start at dawn."

His wife turned swiftly to him and embraced him with an energy that took his breath away. "You," she announced, "are absolutely wonderful! I'm going to tell Miriam right now!"

But at midnight Phyllis slipped into one of her seizures, worse than any either of her parents could remember. Alexander, summoned by Dagon, shook his head. "I don't know," he said. "I'm not sure she'll survive this one. Let me..."

"No!" hissed Doris. "Don't you dare lay a finger on her, you murderer!" She interposed herself between Alexander and the bed where Phyllis writhed, her hands raised in claws. She was plainly prepared to do battle with the physician, should that prove necessary, and Alexander stepped quickly back, his own hands raised in a gesture at once of submission and of calming.

"Peace, Doris!" he said. "I haven't touched her!"

"And you won't either," declared Doris, still in a whisper. "I mean her to live, not die!"

"Good for you," declared the ruffled physician somewhat sardonically. "Since you have, it seems, rejected my offer to provide a safe and comfortable passage hence for Phyllis, what do you propose to do to keep her here in equal comfort and safety? It's all right, Dagon," he added to his friend. "I don't hold it against you, nor am I insulted. I was just trying to help--and I do care about the child, whatever Doris chooses to believe." His tone on the last words was bitter, but the look he gave Dagon affirmed his words, not the bitterness, and Dagon nodded.

"I know you, Alex," he said. "Thank you for trying to help us."

"But what have you planned?" demanded Alexander turning to Doris who still stood guard over her daughter's bed.

"To take her to Jesus from Nazareth to have the demon driven out of her," she snapped at him.

"All the way to Nazareth? She'll never stand the trip," declared the physician flatly.

"No, Alex," Dagon assured him. "Only as far as Joab's house in the village. It seems that's where He's staying."

"Well, you can't take her even that far while the seizure lasts," declared the physician more quietly but no less firmly. "You'll kill her outright. And if you try to move her--how, donkey litter?" he interrupted himself. At Dagon's nod he went on, "that's the best way; but even by donkey litter, if you move her too soon after she comes out of the seizure she could go into another, and each one has been more severe than the one before it. Her heart won't stand two in a row. Besides, the excitement of travel would amplify the effects of this seizure as well as increase the likelihood of a recurrence, even if you did wait long enough."

"How long is 'long enough'?" asked Dagon, seeing the tears begin to gather in his wife's eyes. She had not moved nor relaxed her protective stance, but her husband could see she was badly shaken by having her one hope snatched from her.

"I don't know," said Alexander to his friend, "and I won't take the risk of making a guess at this point. But I am sure you'll kill her if you move her now. Somebody has to stay with her twenty-four hours a day," he added, looking from Miriam to Dagon to Doris.

Since the beginning of the seizure Miriam had been holding Phyllis' tongue down with the ivory depressor Alexander had given Dagon for that purpose. Now she yawned involuntarily. Alexander looked swiftly at her. "You're exhausted, child," he said. "You've had too much. Doris?"

"Dagon always does that," responded the mother, her tears beginning to flow. "I seem to make her nervous whenever I touch her, and the seizure gets worse. I ruin everything for her." She wept, dropping hands and Dagon moved to her, taking her in his arms.

"You must rest, my love," he said quietly. "You know it's not that Phyllis doesn't love you, and not that you don't love her. You are a very good mother, and your not being able to do this one thing doesn't ruin that." His look to the physician was both command and plea and Alexander responded at once.

"Come, Doris," he said briskly. "You must let Dagon relieve Miriam, and you must see to it that Miriam gets some sleep. Then you must sleep, so you can care for them as they help Phyllis through this part of her illness. Then you can go back to her as you have always done... excellently, I might add," he finished warmly.

He had taken no umbrage at Doris' fierce attack upon him; indeed, if it had not come he would have been surprised. He touched her gently and she released Dagon who at once relieved Miriam, holding down the ivory depressor with one hand as he stroked his daughter with the other, talking all the while. His daughter began to grow quiet as his wife had done, and, seeing the change begin, Alexander turned his full attention to Doris.

"Sit down," he said firmly, and she obeyed. He opened his bag full of herbs, selected several, and brought out a small stone mortar and pestle. He crushed the herbs and filled the mortar from the kettle of water bubbling over the charcoal brazier near the open window. After the herbs had steeped he poured the brew into two cups which he brought, steaming, to Miriam and Doris. "Drink up!" he commanded cheerfully, and both women drank obediently, though Doris did sniff once at the steam rising from the cup before she put it to her lips.

"Camomel?" she asked, but without anger or suspicion. It was as though they had never been anything but friends.

"And sassafras," he affirmed, in the same tone he always used. Then, cautiously, he asked, "What will you do now?"

"Wait and see, I suppose," she replied. "Perhaps, if we can't get Phyllis to Jesus, we can persuade Him to come to her. I really think He can heal her, Alex," she added with the same defensiveness that she had used with Dagon.

To her surprise, the physician was nodding quite seriously. "If anyone can," he said simply, "I know I can't. I've done everything I know. That's why I--well, anyway." He took a quick breath. "I've heard about Jesus," he went on, "and I've even seen one of the people He cured, a blind beggar. I always used to give him an alms when I went to see my sister, but he wasn't in his usual place the last time. When I asked about him they brought me to his shop! It was the same man all right, but now he's making harnesses. He told me all about Jesus." He looked at Doris, whose eyes were beginning to close. "Better get some sleep now," he advised. "The sun'll be fully up in two hours, and you'll want to make an early start. Jesus doesn't usually stay in one place long, they say, and you'll want to catch Him before He leaves Joab's, or there's no telling where you'll have to go to track Him down, nor how long it'll take to get Him back here. And we haven't got all that much time, I'm afraid."

She nodded, understanding his words but taking no infection of fear from them, so well had the clever physician's "tea" done its work. Then she slept.

Watching her and Miriam, who was also asleep, Dagon said softly, one eyebrow raised inquiringly, "Camomel and sassafras, Alex?"

"Among other things," his friend said with a grin. "That's what could be tasted and smelled." Then seeing the look of concern in Dagon's face he hastened to add, "Don't worry, Dagon. The only other ingredient in that "tea" was a little poppy. They'll sleep for a couple of hours and be all the better for it. Trust me," he added and looked a question into Dagon's eyes.

"I do." his friend replied simply, meeting his gaze. "With the heart of my heart and my very life. I always have. I always will."

When Phyllis' seizure had ended and she was resting comfortably, Alex departed quietly, leaving Dagon watching the child. Shortly after his departure, Doris woke. "Dagon?" she called and her husband answered.

"With Phyllis," he said softly. "She's out of her seizure and Alex has gone home."

"We don't dare move her, do we?" she asked coming to him.

"No." he answered.

"Then I shall go to Joab's to find Jesus before He continues on His travels. I shall bring Him back with me."

Looking at her, Dagon did not doubt that his wife

would do exactly as she had said. He hoped Jesus would not doubt it either--it would be easier on all of them! "Go in peace, my love," he said. "I'll stay here with Phyllis. Do you want Miriam to go with you?"

"To Joab's? Don't be silly! I can find my own way there and back, and you'll need Miriam's help should Phyllis--should things not go well. I'll be all right. Don't fret over me!" Quickly she kissed him, drew her shawl over her head and was gone.

The day dawned clear. It would be hot later, Doris knew, but now it was fresh and cool. Birds sang. If she hadn't been so anxious, Doris would have enjoyed the walk and the solitude. As it was, she hurried along, concentrating on taking the shortest way to Joab's and thinking about what she would say once she got there.

As it turned out, she needn't have worried. Nearing the street where Joab lived, Doris ran into the outer edges of a crowd. She knew from the reports Miriam's "network" had supplied that such crowds usually gathered whenever Jesus set foot out of doors, and that on occasion they had mobbed the places where He stayed, not doing damage but certainly announcing the presence of the wonderworker.

Now which one was He? Rapidly scanning what she could see of the boiling crowd Miriam felt her heart drop. How could she locate one man in all that mob when she had never seen Him before and could not, with certainty, find the crowd's center from the corner where she had gotten herself wedged? What could she do?

Doris refused to allow the wave of futility and despair that she sensed was ready to engulf her even to form itself in her receptive imagination. That would be no use to Phyllis or her--and it surely wouldn't help in finding Jesus.

As she searched for a way out of her dilemma a sound caught her attention. Rising above the blur of crowd noise, a child's wail cut a clean path into the attention of every adult within earshot. "Mama!" wailed the little one, and everyone around him turned.

Through the crowd his description raced, and within three minutes his mother came, hurrying as the people squeezed aside to let her through, to sweep him into her arms, embrace him, cover him with kisses and then spank him briskly for having wandered off from her side in the first place. The spanking ended with a hug and a kiss, and mother and son edged their way out of the crowd and walked off together harmoniously.

"Too bad I can't do that!" thought Doris and then stopped short. "Why can't I do just exactly that? I might look like a fool, but I'd find Him--and that's the point!" At once she threw back her shawl raised her head, and, at the top of her lungs cried out, "Son of David! Son of David! Son of David!"

As had happened for the child, the crowd turned toward her and then in the direction where Jesus was. She saw the movement, and still crying out, "Son of David!" she began to move that way. The crowd parted to let her through, some of them even pointing out the right direction to her, and others clearing her way.

"She wants to get to Jesus! Let her through," said several, and very soon she found herself at the center of the crowd.

Continuing her ear-shattering chant, Doris rapidly assessed the people at this knot in the crowd. They seemed to be focused around one gentle-seeming man, looking to him as she called out, so, looking at him too, she cried, "Son of David! Have mercy on me, sir! My daughter has a demon and is in a terrible condition."

He had heard her, Doris knew. For an instant His eyes met hers, and the touch of His compassion was a kind of healing she had never known.

But then His gaze was hooded and He seemed to draw back inside Himself, though in fact He did not even shift His weight from one foot to the other. He must not go! He must not escape or be lost! He must heal Phyllis!

More loudly than before Doris called again, "Son of David! Son of David! Son of David!" But He had turned away and begun to move off. She was desperate. Here was Phyllis' life pouring out into the sand because she could not compel this Jesus to heal the child.

As Doris continued to cry out with ever-mounting urgency, she saw His followers speak to Him. She heard them say to Jesus, "Send her away! She is following us and making all this noise!"

"Good!" thought Doris as she repeated her cry with even more energy. "If He tries to send me away, maybe I can get close enough to Him to catch His hand. And then I can drag Him to Phyllis if I have to!"

She moved a little closer, pushing someone. She cried out again, and heard Him say, ostensibly to His followers but really, she knew, to her, "I have been sent only to the lost sheep of the house of Israel." There was a note of apology in His voice and His eyes met hers again with that wondrous healing touch.

Suddenly a path opened in front of her and she rushed down it, flinging herself at Jesus' feet, fully prepared to wrap her strong arms around His knees if He tried to move away. "Help me, sir!" she gasped.

Jesus looked down at her for a long minute. He seemed to enter into her pain and to take it upon Himself, for His eyes darkened under suddenly fur-rowed brows and His mouth contracted even as she felt within herself a sudden easing of tension and the first flooding in of peace. She stayed perfectly still and look-ed her plea at Him, her heart speaking through her eyes.

It was Jesus who broke the silence. In a strangely familiar tone which she could not quite place He said, "It isn't right to take the children's food and throw it to the dogs."

The words were an insult, the traditional one used by Jews dealing with or discussing non-Jews, Doris knew. Dogs. So Gentiles seemed to these people "chosen" by their God. Ordinarily Doris would have been furious or contemptuous. But now she was not. Jesus had used insulting words, but He was not insulting her or her daughter. He had given the Jew's argument against helping a Gentile, and He was waiting for her to say something, hoping she would think of the thing to say that would overturn the "reasonable" argument and allow Him to do what He wanted to do as much as she wanted Him to do it. But He would not act without that word, and she could not think what it was.

In the long minute that followed, Doris' mind refused to work. Instead, her memory started tossing colored balls of random associations at her, as Dagon used to tease Phyllis before she learned to catch a ball. Jesus even sounded like Dagon, she thought--so reasonable and so prevented by his own reasoning from doing what he really wanted to do.

Thinking of Dagon, she thought also of Spot and Brownie, and her own frustration at being unable to keep Phyllis from feeding them at the table. Poor dogs, they missed Phyllis, and not just for her table scraps.

Suddenly her mind stopped short. There it was! She had the reason Jesus wanted her to find. A smile like the blaze of the summer sun broke over her face. With Dagon's measured, judicious tones in her ear she repeated the dictum he had given that had solved Spot and Brownie's problem. "That's true, sir," she answered him, a clarion of joy sounding in her voice, because she knew she was setting them all free, "but even the dogs eat the family's table scraps!"

The blaze of her joy was met and matched by His own. As if a weight had been lifted from Him He smiled back at her. "You are a woman of great faith!" He declared. "What you want will be done for you! Go back home, where you will find that the demon has gone out of your daughter!"

At once Doris rose. She stood for an instant facing Him, her whole body expressing gratitude and joy more clearly than words could ever have done. She bowed deeply to Him, met His eyes again, and at His slight nod, turned and began to run through the swiftly parting crowd, back the way she had come.

She ran most of the way to her home, slowing to a walk only when her breath gave out, and then running

again, running and running. She turned up the path
to home some forty minutes after she had left Jesus,
and Dagon, tears running down his face met her at the
door.

'She is well! Phyllis is well!" he kept saying over
and over as he embraced her.

"When?" she asked, pulling back when she had
gotten her breath back.

"About forty minutes ago," her husband replied, and
Doris threw back her head and laughed, raising her
arms high in the air.

"Praise God!" she shouted. "Praise Jesus!" Then
she grabbed Dagon's hands and began to dance him
vigorously around the front yard. "He did it! Jesus did
it! He did it with His word alone!" she caroled, and
then pulled Dagon with her into the house. "Where's
Miriam?" she was asking. "I've got to tell you both all
about it!"

The door shut behind them as they went in together.
In the yard, Spot raised his head. Brownie, hearing
him bark, came from around the house. Together the
dogs moved to the kitchen door where they settled side
by side to wait for Phyllis and their supper.